Atki

New Complete Cookbook 2022

365 Days of Super, Easy & Healthy Recipes to Burn Fat, Loss Weight and Boost Energy

By

Andrew Modimo Mclaggan

Table of Contents

INTRODUCTION OF ATKINS DIET

Atkins weight loss program is a excessive-protein, excessive-fats, low-sugar weight reduction eating regimen. Atkins takes into attention unhindered measures of meat, cheddar, and eggs whilst seriously limiting starches, inclusive of sugar, bread, pasta, milk, products of the soil. The Atkins weight-reduction plan depends on the speculation that consuming sugars invigorates the generation of insulin, which consequently prompts appetite, consuming, and weight benefit. The hypothesis is that people on the Atkins weight loss plan revel in reduced hunger and their bodies use to place away fat for power rather than ingesting glucose from ingested sugar.

Consuming fat for power is probably lead to weight loss.

On the positive aspect of the file, people on the Atkins food plan typically like eating the high measures of protein sustenance's that might be restricted on unique consuming regimens. The individuals who have been fruitless on other low-fat, high-starch eats much less often get in form on the Atkins eating regimen. The eating habitual is whatever but difficult to pursue. No factor framework, calorie tallying or harassed supper plans are blanketed.

- **Low-Carb Diets Reduce Your Appetite:**

Yearning will in the present day be the maximum highly lousy response of abstaining from excessive food consumption. It is one of the primary motives why several individuals sense hopeless and in the end surrender.

Notwithstanding low-carb ingesting activates a programmed lower in hunger. Concentrates reliably showcase that when humans reduce carbs and consume more protein and fats, they grow to be consuming an extended manner an awful lot fewer energy.

- **Weight Loss at First:**

Cutting carbs is one of the easiest and excellent techniques to get in shape. Studies define that people on low-carb abstains from food lose more weight, quicker, than the ones on low-fats consuming regimens notwithstanding while the closing is efficaciously confining energy.

This is when you consider that low-carb slims down act to free abundance water out of your frame, bringing insulin ranges and driving down to rapid weight reduction within the principal week or two. In studies contrasting low-carb and low-fats consuming regimens, individuals confining their carbs sometimes lose 2– 3 fold the quantity of weight without being starving.

One exam in huge grown-America observed a low-carb diet especially possible for as long as half of the year, contrasted with an everyday weight loss food plan. From that factor forward, the difference in weight loss between eating regimens became unimportant. In yr-long research in 609 overweight grown-united states of American low-fat or low-carb eat fewer carbs, the two gatherings lost similar measures of weight.

- **Fat Loss Comes From Abdominal Cavity:**

Not all fat on your body is equal. Where fats are positioned away makes a decision about how it impacts your well-being and chance of contamination.

The fundamental kinds are subcutaneous fat that is beneath your pores and skin and instinctive fat, which aggregates in your stomach melancholy and is normal for maximum overweight guys. Instinctive fat will in general lodge around your organs. Overabundance instinctive fat is associated with infection and insulin competition and might drive the metabolic brokenness so ordinary in the West nowadays.

Low-carb consumes much fewer calories are extremely compelling at reducing this hurtful stomach fat. Actually, a more outstanding quantity of the husky individuals lose on low-carb consumes much less energy appears to originate from the stomach pit.

After some time, this needs to spark off a considerably decreased risk of coronary infection and sort 2 diabetes.

- **Triglycerides Tend to Drop Drastically:**

Triglycerides are fat debris that circles for your circulatory device. It is outstanding that excessive fasting triglycerides ranges in the blood after a medium-time period short are a strong coronary infection chance issue. One of the essential drivers of raised triglycerides in inactive individuals is carb usage particularly the primary sugar fructose.

At the factor, while individuals reduce carbs, they'll in general revel in an exceedingly emotional decrease in blood triglycerides.

Then again, low-fats weight manipulates plans frequently reason triglycerides to increment.

- **Expanded Levels of 'Good' HDL Cholesterol:**

High-thickness lipoprotein (HDL) is regularly referred to as the "awesome" LDL cholesterol. The higher your dimensions of HDL in recognize to "awful" LDL, the decrease your risk of coronary illness.

A standout among the maximum best tactics to build "super" HDL degrees is to consume fat and coffee-carb abstains from food comprise a ton of fat.

In this manner, it is apparent that HDL ranges increment drastically on strong, low-carb slims down, whilst they will in preferred increment just respectably or maybe decay on low-fat weight management plans.

- **Diminished Blood Sugar and Insulin Levels:**

Low-carb and ketogenic diets can likewise be especially beneficial for people with diabetes and insulin opposition, which impact a massive range of people around the arena.

Studies demonstrate that cutting carbs brings down each glucose and insulin levels definitely.

A few human beings with diabetes who begin a low-carb weight-reduction plan may additionally need to lessen their insulin dose via half of right away.

In one investigation in individuals with type 2 diabetes, 95% had dwindled or worn out their glucose-bringing down prescription interior a 1/2 yr.

In the occasion which you take glucose medicinal drug, communicate along with your specialist before making adjustments for your carb admission, as your dose may additionally be acclimated to counteract hypoglycemia.

- **May Lower Blood Pressure:**

Raised circulatory pressure, or hypertension, is a crucial risk element for a few, infections, which include coronary contamination, stroke and kidney unhappiness.

Low-carb slims down are a hit method to bring down circulatory stress, which should decrease your chance of those illnesses and assist you to live extra.

- **Viable Against Metabolic Syndrome:**

The metabolic ailment is a circumstance very related to your hazard of diabetes and coronary illness.

Truth be told, metabolic disease is an accumulation of manifestations, which include:

- ✓ Stomach weight
- ✓ Raised circulatory strain
- ✓ Raised fasting glucose ranges
- ✓ High triglycerides
- ✓ Low "exceptional" HDL levels of cholesterol
- ✓ In any case, a low-carb weight-reduction plan is particularly compelling in treating each one of the five of these facet outcomes.

- ✓ Under such a weight-reduction plan, those situations are almost disbursed with.

- ➢ **Improved 'Awful' LDL Cholesterol Levels:**

Individuals who've high "awful" LDL are substantially extra at risk of having coronary heart attacks.

Be that as it could, the quantity of the debris is imperative. Littler debris is connected to a higher hazard of coronary contamination, while bigger debris is connected to decrease risk.

Things being what they're, low-carb eats fewer carbs increment the volume of "lousy" LDL particles while reducing the number of absolute LDL particles on your circulatory machine. Accordingly, bringing down your carb admission can guide your coronary heart well-being.

- ➢ **Restorative for Several Brain Disorders:**

Your thoughts wish glucose, as positive portions of it could just consume this type of sugar. That is the reason your liver produces glucose from protein inside the occasion which you don't consume any carbs.

However, an expansive piece of your cerebrum can likewise consume ketones, that are framed amid hunger or whilst carb admission is rather low.

This is the system at the back of the ketogenic eating regimen, which has been applied for pretty a long time to deal with epilepsy in kids who do not react to tranquilize treatment.

Much of the time, this ingesting routine can fix the offspring of epilepsy. In one investigation, over part of the youngsters on a ketogenic food regimen encountered a greater noteworthy than half decrease in their variety of seizures, even as 16% moved towards turning into without seizure. Low-carb and ketogenic consumes less energy are presently being focused for other mind situations also, along with Alzheimer's and Parkinson's contamination

Herbed chicken and mushrooms

Prep Time: 25mins, Cooking Time: 30mins, Servings :4

INGREDIENTS

- 8 - skin-on chicken thighs
- 2 - teaspoons sea salt
- ½ - teaspoon black pepper
- 2 - tablespoon dried oregano
- 2 - tablespoon dried thyme
- 2 - tablespoon dried rosemary
- 2 - tablespoons olive oil
- 8 - ounces cremini mushrooms, quartered
- 2 - cloves garlic, minced
- 1 - cup chicken stock
- 2 - tablespoons Dijon mustard
- Torn fresh parsley, optional as garnish

INSTRUCTIONS

- Preheat the broiler to 400°F.
- Season the chook thighs on the two facets with salt, pepper, 2 teaspoons of the oregano, 2 teaspoons of the dried thyme, and a couple of teaspoons of the dried rosemary.
- Warmth the olive oil in an expansive cast iron skillet over medium warm temperature. Add the chook to the skillet, pores and skin aspect down.
- Flip the chicken thighs over to the alternative facet and exchange the skillet to the stove. Prepare for 15 to 20mins, till the fowl is cooked absolutely through.

- Move the skillet lower back to the stovetop. Expel the chook from the box, positioned apart, and spread to hold warm.
- To a similar skillet, encompass the mushrooms and prepare dinner over medium warmth for five minutes, till they've discharged their fluid and are delicate.
- Include the garlic, fowl inventory, Dijon mustard, and the relaxation of the seasonings and prepare dinner for an extra 3 minutes.
- Plate the hen and pour the sauce over great. Trimming with crisp parsley, every time wanted.
- **Nutrition Information:** Calories 127g, Fat 1.5g, Carbs 0.5g, Sugars 0.3g, Protein 26.3g

Low carb whole30 almond coconut milk creamer

Prep Time: 10mins, Cooking Time: 10mins, Servings :1

INGREDIENTS

- 2 - cups raw almonds
- 2 - cups filtered water
- 14.5 - ounce can organic coconut cream
- 2 - teaspoons pure vanilla extract

INSTRUCTIONS

- Douse the crude almond overnight, shrouded in water. They will decrease and full. Dispose of the water.
- Spot the almonds in an effective blender with 2 mugs crisp water, coconut cream and vanilla listen. Mix on high for 2 minutes.
- Spot a piece strainer over a bowl or a widespread estimating container. Spot a substantial nut sack over the sifter. Empty the almond combination into the nut sack and permit it to strain through into the bowl.
- Close the nut percent and curve across the almond mash and press. Press immovably into the strainer to separate however much milk as could moderately be predicted.
- Keep in the refrigerator for at least seven days.

Nutrition Information: Calories 138g, Fat 14.3g, Carbs 3.3g, Sugars 2g, Protein 1.4g

Paleo 2 minute avocado oil mayo

Prep Time: 15mins, Cooking Time: 10mins, Servings :2

INGREDIENTS

- 2 - teaspoons lemon juice
- 1 - large egg
- ½ - teaspoon dry mustard powder
- ½ - teaspoon sea salt
- 1 - cup avocado oil

INSTRUCTIONS

- To a tall, wide mouth artisan container include the lemon squeeze first, at that point the egg, seasonings, lastly the oil. Give the fixings a chance to rest for 20 seconds or somewhere in the vicinity.
- Put the drenching blender the whole distance at the base of the artisan container. Turn it on fast and abandon it at the base of the container for around 20 seconds. The mayonnaise will promptly start to set up and fill the container.
- After the mayonnaise is practically the whole distance set, gradually pull the drenching blender towards the highest point of the container without removing the edges from the mayonnaise. At that point, gradually drive it back towards the base of the container. Rehash this stage two or multiple times until the majority of the fixings are well all around consolidated.
- Taste and include increasingly salt, whenever wanted.

Nutrition Information: Calories 109g, Fat 12.2g, Carbs 0.1g, Sugar 0.2, Protein 0.5g

LOW CARB TACO CASSEROLE

Prep Time: 25mins, Cooking Time: 30mins, Servings :8

INGREDIENTS

- 1 - pound ground beef
- ¼ - cup chopped onion
- 1 - jalapeno minced
- 1 - packet taco seasoning
- ¼ - cup water, 2 - ounces cream cheese
- ¼ - cup salsa, 4 - eggs
- 1 - tablespoon hot sauce
- ¼ - cup heavy whipping cream
- ½ - cup grated cheddar
- ½ - cup grated pepperjack cheese

INSTRUCTIONS

- Preheat broiler to 350 degrees. Shower an 8x8 preparing dish with the non-stick splash.
- Dark colored the ground hamburger in a huge skillet over medium warmth.
- Add the onions and jalapeno to the meat and cook until onion is translucent. Channel any oil.
- Mix in the taco flavoring and water and cook for 5 minutes.
- Include the cream cheddar and salsa and mix to join.
- Break the eggs in a medium bowl and race with the hot sauce and overwhelming cream.
- Pour the meat blend into the readied preparing dish and best with the egg blend.
- Sprinkle with cheddar and heat for 30 minutes or until eggs are set.
- Cool 5 minutes before cutting and serving.

Nutrition Information: Calories 419.9g, Fat 33.9g, Carbs 2.9g, Sugars 1g, Protein 24.2g

Spinach and Mushroom Breakfast Casserole

Prep Time: 35mins, Cooking Time: 35mins, Servings :6

Ingredients

- 12 - ounce bag fresh baby spinach
- 1/2 - lb. mushrooms sliced
- 3 - green onions sliced, 1 - medium onion chopped
- 2 - cloves garlic minced, 6 - eggs beaten
- 5 - Tablespoons unsalted butter divided
- 16 - oz. cottage cheese
- 12 - ounces sharp cheddar cheese grated
- 1 - teaspoon kosher salt
- ½ - teaspoon black pepper

Instructions

- Pre-heat broiler to 350* F. Utilizes 1 Tablespoon spread to grease 13" X nine" heating dish.
- Warmth 4 Tablespoons margarine in an intensive skillet or sauté container, and sauté onions, mushrooms, and garlic for 3-4 of minutes until onions are translucent and mushrooms are delicate.
- Include spinach, a group at any given second, and sauté. Spread skillet and allow spinach decrease, round 5mins.
- Give cool, a risk to empty abundance fluid, and hack all the greater finely every time desired.
- In a special bowl, whisk eggs, curds, cheddar, and salt and pepper. Include cooked spinach and mushroom combination.

- Blend properly and fill making ready dish.
- Heat for 45-50mins or until fine is tremendous darkish colored and attention is finished.

Nutrition Information: Calories 193.6g, Fat 14.2g, Carbs 3.8g, Sugars 2.1g, Protein 12.8g

Alfredo Sauce Recipe

Prep Time: 25mins, Cooking Time: 25mins, Servings :4

INGREDIENTS

- 2 - tablespoons Unsalted Butter Stick
- 1 ½ - cups Heavy Cream
- ½ - cup Parmesan Cheese (Grated)
- 4 - oz Romano Cheese
- 1/8 - tsp Black Pepper,
- 1/8 - tsp Nutmeg (Ground)

instructions

- Liquefy margarine in a medium pot over medium warmth. Include cream and stew until diminished to 1 glass, around 10 minutes. Mesh Parmesan and Romano cheeses.
- Pour from warmth; blend in Parmesan, Romano, pepper and nutmeg until the cheeses have softened and sauce is smooth.
- Serve promptly.

Nutrition Information: Calories 349.1g, Fat 31g, Carbs 7.7g, Sugars 0.2g, Protein 11.6g

Almond & Coconut Flour Muffin in a Mug

Prep Time: 35mins, Cooking Time: 25mins, Servings :1

INGREDIENTS

- 2 - tbsps Almond Meal Flour
- 1/3 - tbsp Organic High Fiber Coconut Flour
- 1 - teaspoon Sucralose Based Sweetener (Sugar Substitute)
- ½ - tsp Cinnamon
- ¼ - tsp Baking Powder (Straight Phosphate, Double Acting)
- 1/8 - tsp Salt
- 1 - large Egg
- 1 - tsp Extra Virgin Olive Oil

Instructions

- Spot every dry fixing in an espresso cup. Blend to consolidate.
- Include the egg and oil. Mix until completely consolidated.
- Microwave for 1 minute. Utilize a blade if important to help cut the biscuit off from the glass, cut, and margarine, eat.

Nutrition Information: Calories 204.6g, Fat 18.4g, Carbs 8.1g, Sugars 0.4g, Protein6.1g

2 Ingredient Low Carb Crepes

Prep Time: 35mins, Cooking Time: 20mins, Servings :6

INGREDIENTS

- For the batter, 2 - oz cream cheese full fat
- 2 – eggs, Topping (optional)
- ½ - cup mixed berries
- 2 - tbsp heavy whipping cream
- Low Carb Crepes

INSTRUCTIONS

- Warm up cream cheddar in a microwave so it motivates delicate and simple to blend
- Add 2 eggs to cream cheddar (each one in turn) and blend well. Utilize a hand blender or a whisk. Add any flavors to the blend (discretionary)
- Warm up a skillet, oil it marginally (I put some oil on an abundance and cleaned my skillet) and make your crepes.
- Discretionary: You can make it sweet by including whipped cream, strawberries, berries, Greek yogurt, maple syrup and cinnamon. (Ensure it accommodates your macros.

Nutrition Information: Calories 116.4g, Fat 5.3g, Carbs 11.9g, Sugars 6.2g, Protein 6.7g

Stuffed Chicken with Asparagus & Bacon

Prep Time: 5mins, Cooking Time: 40mins, Servings: 4

Ingredients

- 8 - chicken tenders about 1 lb
- ½ - tsp salt , ¼ - tsp pepper
- 12 - asparagus spears about .5 lb
- 8 - pieces bacon about .5 lb

Instructions

- Preheat oven to 400.
- Spot 2 chook tenders to complete the system of the whole lot.
- Season with pretty salt and pepper.
- Incorporate three spears of asparagus.
- Overlay the bacon over the fowl and asparagus to shield each and every piece of it together.
- Warmth for 40mins until the hen is cooked through, the asparagus is clean, and the bacon is new.

Nutrition Information: Calories 377g, Fat 25g, Carbs 3g, Sugars 1g, Protein 32g

BASIL STUFFED CHICKEN BREASTS

Prep Time: 20mins, Cooking Time: 45mins, Servings : 4

INGREDIENTS

- 2 - bone-in, skin-on chicken breasts, 2 - tbs cream cheese
- 2 - tbs shredded cheese, ¼ - tsp garlic paste
- 3-4 - fresh basil leaves finely chopped, black pepper

INSTRUCTIONS

- Preheat the oven to 375F.
- Make the stuffing by joining the cream cheddar, cheddar, garlic paste, basil, and dull pepper.
- Carefully strip back the skin on one side of the chicken chest and detect the half stuffing inside.
- Smooth it down and supersede the skin
- Repeat for the other piece of chicken.
- Cook on a getting ready plate for 45 minutes or until the inward temperature of 165F has been come to.

Nutrition Information: Calories 152g, Fat 15g, Carbs 8g, Sugar 12g, Protein 22g

Low Carb Pork Medallions

Prep Time: 15mins, Cooking Time: 30mins, Servings : 4

Ingredients

- 1 - lb. pork tenderloin
- 3 - medium shallots (chopped nice), ¼ - cup oil

Instructions

- Diminish the hamburger into half-inch thick cuts.
- hack the shallots and notice them on a plate.
- warm the oil in a skillet press each and every piece of red meat into the shallots on the 2 angles.
- Detect the hamburger cuts with shallots into the warm oil and get ready supper till achieved.
- You will find that a piece of the shallots will expend for the span of cooking, at the same time, they'll even now present delightful taste to the meat.
- Essentially cook supper the red meat until it's cooked through.
- Present with veggies.

Nutrition Information: Calories 53g, Fat 5g, Carbs 1g, Sugar 2g, Protein 6g

Easy Mozzarella & Pesto Chicken Casserole

Prep Time: 30mins, Cooking Time: 30mins, Servings : 4

Ingredients

- ¼ - cup pesto, 8 - oz cream cheese softened
- ¼ - ½ - cup heavy cream
- 8 - oz mozzarella cubed
- 2 - lb cooked cubed chicken breasts
- 8 - oz mozzarella shredded

Instructions

- Preheat stove to 400. Sprinkle a tremendous supper dish with cooking shower.
- Unite the underlying three fixings and mix until smooth in a broad bowl.
- Incorporate the chicken and cubed mozzarella. Trade to the goulash dish.
- Sprinkle the decimated mozzarella to complete the process of everything.
- Plan for 25-30 minutes. Present with zoodles, spinach, or squashed cauliflower

Nutrition Information: Calories 452g, Fat 26g, Carbs 11g, Sugars 5g, Protein 39g

Broccoli & Cheddar Keto Bread Recipe

Prep Time: 20mins, Cooking Time: 35mins, Servings: 8

Ingredients

- 5 - eggs beaten, 1 - cup shredded cheddar cheese
- ¾ - cup fresh raw broccoli florets chopped
- 3 ½ - tbsp coconut flour, 2 - tsp baking powder, 1 - tsp salt

Instructions

- Preheat broiler to 350. Shower a portion skillet with a cooking splash.
- Blend every one of the fixings in a medium bowl. Fill the portion skillet.
- Heat for 30-35 minutes or until puffed and brilliant. Cut and serve.
- To Reheat Microwave or warmth in a lubed griddle.

Nutrition Information: Calories 443g, Fat 29.8g, Carbs 5.8g, Sugars 2.1g, Protein 37.2g

Bacon Wrapped Chicken Tenders with Ranch Dip

Prep Time: 20mins, Cooking Time: 35mins, Servings :12

Ingredients:

- 12- chicken tenderloins about 1.5 lb, 12 - slices of bacon
- Ranch Dip Ingredients:
- 1/3 - cup sour cream, 1/3 - cup mayo, ½ - tsp salt
- 1 - tsp each garlic powder onion powder, parsley, and dill

Instructions

- Preheat the broiler to 400.
- Wrap every chicken delicate firmly in a bit of bacon. I extended the bacon as I folded it over the chicken.
- Spot on a heating sheet. Prepare for 35-45 minutes until the bacon is fresh and the chicken is completely cooked.
- In the meantime, mix together the elements for the plunge. Present with the cooked chicken.

Nutrition Information: Calories 204g, Fat 15g, Carbs 0.1g, Sugar 3.2g, Protein 13g

Farmhouse Beans & Sausage

Prep Time: 15mins, Cooking Time: 30mins, Servings :3

Ingredients

- 2 - cups gluten-free chicken broth
- 2 16 - oz. frozen green beans
- 1 16 - oz. chicken sausage, sliced
- ½ - onion, diced
- 2 - teaspoons Herbamare
- salt & pepper to taste

Instructions

- Spot all fixings in the Instant Pot. Spot top on and close ensuring the steam vent is shut.
- Utilize manual setting and set at 6 minutes.
- At the point when cook time is done utilize the fast discharge strategy to let off the steam.

Nutrition Information: Calories 297.6g, Fat 8.2g, Carbs 38.2g, Sugars 4.8g, Protein 19.4g

Meat-Lover Pizza Cups

Prep Time: 15mins, Cooking Time: 35mins, Servings :12

Ingredients

- 12 - deli ham slices
- 1 - lb. bulk Italian sausage
- 12 - Tbsp sugar-free pizza sauce
- 3 - cups grated mozzarella cheese
- 24 - pepperoni slices
- 1 - cup cooked and crumbled bacon

Instructions

- Preheat stove to 375 F. Dark colored Italian frankfurter in skillet, depleting abundance oil.
- Line 12-container biscuit tin with ham cuts. Gap frankfurter, pizza sauce, mozzarella cheddar, pepperoni cuts, and bacon disintegrate between each container, in a specific order.
- Prepare at 375 for 10 minutes. Cook for 1 minute until cheddar air pockets and tans and the edges of the meat garnishes look firm.
- Take pizza containers out from biscuit tin and set on paper towel to keep the bottoms from getting wet. Appreciate promptly or refrigerate and re-heat in toaster broiler or microwave.

Nutrition Information: Calories 520g, Fat 29g, Carbs 38g, Sugars 4g, Protein 26g

5 Minute 5 Ingredient Cheesy Bacon Chicken

Prep Time: 10mins, Cooking Time: 40mins, Servings :6

Ingredients

- 5 to 6 - chicken breasts , cut in half width wise
- 2 - tbsp seasoning rub
- ½ - pound bacon , cut strips in half
- 4 - oz shredded cheddar
- sugar free barbecue sauce , optional, to serve

Instructions

- Preheat stove to 400. Splash a huge rimmed preparing sheet with cooking shower.
- Rub the two sides of chicken bosoms with flavoring rub. Top each with a bit of bacon. Prepare for 30 min on the best rack until the chicken is 160 degrees and the bacon looks firm.
- Take plate out from the broiler and sprinkle the cheddar over the bacon. Set back in the broiler for around 10 min until the cheddar is bubbly and brilliant. Present with grill sauce.

Nutrition Information: Calories 345g, Fat 23g, Carbs 1g, Sugar 4.1g, Protein 29g

Baked Pesto Chicken

Prep Time: 20mins, Cooking Time: 40mins, Servings :4

Ingredients

- 4 - chicken breasts about 1.5 lb, sliced in half widthwise to make 8 pieces
- 3 - tbsp basil pesto
- 8 - oz mozzarella thinly sliced or shredded
- ½ - tsp salt, ¼ - tsp black pepper

Instructions

- Preheat stove to 350.
- Splash making a ready dish with cooking shower. Spot chicken inside the base in a solitary layer and sprinkle with the salt and pepper. Spread the pesto on the bird. Put the mozzarella to finish everything.
- Prepare for 35-forty five minutes till the chook is a hundred and sixty stages and the cheddar is excellent and bubbly. You can sear it for a few minutes toward the conclusion to darker the cheddar inside the event that you want.

Nutrition Information: Calories 287.5g, Fat 16g, Carbs 4.3g, Sugars 1.8g, Protein 30.3g

Pizza Chicken Casserole

Prep Time: 15mins, Cooking Time: 30mins, Servings :4

Ingredients

- 1.5 to 2 - lb cooked chicken breast sliced or cubed
- 8 - oz cream cheese
- 1 - tsp dried minced garlic
- 1 - cup marinara sauce no sugar added
- 8 - oz shredded mozzarella

Instructions

- Preheat oven to 350.
- Put chicken in the backside of a 9x13 baking dish.
- Combine cream cheese and garlic. Drop small spoonfuls onto the bird. Pour the sauce on pinnacle. Sprinkle with the shredded mozzarella.
- Bake for 30 min or till the cheese is melted and bubbly.

Nutrition Information: Calories 258.1g, Fat 14.1g, Carbs 3.1g, Sugars 0.7g, Protein 28.1g

keto cauliflower au gratin

Prep Time: 25mins, Cooking Time: 55mins, Servings :4

INGREDIENTS

- 1 - large head of cauliflower, trimmed and cut into florets
- 2 - small red onions, thinly sliced
- 2 - tablespoons olive oil
- 2 - tablespoons balsamic vinegar
- 1 - tablespoon granular erythritol
- ¾ - cup heavy cream
- ½ - cup finely grated parmesan
- ½ - teaspoon sea salt, more to taste
- ¼ - teaspoon black pepper, more to taste
- 1 - cup shredded gruyere or gouda cheese

INSTRUCTIONS

- Preheat the broiler to 350°F.
- Warmth the olive oil in a significant skillet over medium warmth. When the dish is hot, upload the onions to the field and cook dinner till delicate and sensitive, round 15mins.
- Include the balsamic vinegar and erythritol if utilizing, to the field with the onions, and blend to consolidate. Cook for a further 5 minutes.
- Upload cauliflower florets to the pan and blend it with the onions.
- In a touch bowl, be part of the large cream, parmesan cheddar, salt, and pepper. pour the aggregate over great of the cauliflower.
- Sprinkle the gruyere over high-quality and prepare for 40 minutes or until the cauliflower is touchy and the splendid is first-rate dark colored and bubbly.

Nutrition Information: Calories 230g, Fat 17g, Carbs 11.9g, Sugars 0.4g, Protein 9.2g

boosted keto coffee

Prep Time: 15mins, Cooking Time: 30mins, Servings :1

INGREDIENTS

- 8 - ounces dark roast coffee
- 1 - tablespoons butter flavored coconut oil
- 1 - scoop Keto Zone French Vanilla
- 1 - scoop Collagen Peptides
- 2 - teaspoons monk fruit sweetened caramel syrup
- Splash coconut milk

INSTRUCTIONS

- Pour all the ingredients into a blender or milk frother and Blend till smooth and creamy. ENJOY!!

Nutrition Information: Calories 296g, Fat 23g, Carbs 16g, Sugars 2.1g, Protein 15g

Sugar free low carb dried cranberries

Prep Time: 35mins, Cooking Time: 3hrs 10mins, Servings :1

INGREDIENTS

- 2 to 12 - ounce bags fresh cranberries
- 1 - cup granular erythritol
- 3 - tablespoons avocado oil
- ½ - teaspoon pure orange extract

INSTRUCTIONS

- Preheat the stove to 200°F. Line two rimmed preparing sheets with material paper.
- Wash and dry the cranberries and expel any sautéed or delicate berries. Cut the cranberries into equal parts and add them to a blending bowl.
- Include the sugar, avocado oil, and orange concentrate, if utilizing. Hurl to equitably coat the majority of the berries.
- Line the berries in single layers over the heating sheets.
- Heat for 3 to 4 hours, turning the racks part of the way through.

Nutrition Information: Calories 208.8g, Fat 22.5g, Carbs 0.8g, Sugars 0.1g, Protein 1.6g

keto hollandaise

Prep Time: 15mins, Cooking Time: 20mins, Servings :1

INGREDIENTS

- 4 - egg yolks, 2 - tablespoons fresh lemon juice
- ½ - cup butter (1 stick), melted, dash hot sauce
- pinch of cayenne pepper, pinch of sea salt

INSTRUCTIONS

- In a hardened metallic blending bowl, whisk the egg yolks and lemon squeeze collectively. The mixture need to get thicker and increment in quantity.
- Warmth a pan with 1 to two crawls of water in it over medium warmth until the water is stewing. Lower the warm temperature to medium-low. Spot the bowl over quality of the pan, ensuring that the water is not contacting the bottom of the bowl in any other case the eggs will begin to scramble. Keep whisking fast.
- Gradually, speed within the liquefied spread until the sauce has thickened and is light and cushioned.
- Take it out from the warm temperature and tenderly velocity within the warm sauce, cayenne pepper and ocean salt.

Nutrition Information: Calories 265g, Fat 27g, Carbs 11.2g, Sugars 3g, Protein 5.5g

Dairy free keto ranch dressing

Prep Time: 5mins, Cooking Time: 10mins, Servings :2

INGREDIENTS

- 1 - cup mayonnaise , ¼ - cup water
- 2 - teaspoons chopped fresh chives
- 1 ½ - teaspoons fresh lemon juice
- 1 - teaspoon Dijon mustard
- 1 - teaspoon chopped fresh dill weed
- 1 - teaspoon chopped fresh flat-leaf parsley
- 1 - teaspoon garlic powder
- ½ - teaspoon onion powder
- ½ - teaspoon sea salt, ½ - teaspoon black pepper

INSTRUCTIONS

- Combine all elements together in a mason jar, cap, and shake to mix. Alternately, you may integrate all of the ingredients together in a mixing bowl, and whisk until well integrated.
- Store within the fridge for up to 2 weeks. (If it lasts that long)

Nutrition Information: Calories 132g, Fat 9g, Carbs 8g, Sugar 2.3, Protein 11g

Creamy chive blue cheese dressing

Prep Time: 25mins, Cooking Time: 15mins, Servings :16

INGREDIENTS

- 1 - cup mayonnaise
- ½ - cup sour cream
- 1 - tablespoon fresh lemon juice
- 1 - teaspoon Worcestershire sauce
- 1 - teaspoon garlic powder
- ½ - teaspoon sea salt
- ½ - teaspoon black pepper
- ¾ - cup crumbled blue cheese
- ¼ - cup chopped fresh chives

INSTRUCTIONS

- Pour all ingredients to a medium bowl or container, and mix until well combined.

Nutrition Information: Calories 106g, Fat 12g, Carbs 1g, Sugar 0.4, Protein 1g

Black beauty – low carb vodka drink

Prep Time: 10mins, Cooking Time: 5mins, Servings :1

INGREDIENTS

- 2 - ounces vodka
- 5 - fresh blackberries
- ¾ - ounce fresh lemon juice (1 ½ tablespoons)
- 2 - teaspoons powdered erythritol
- ¼ - teaspoon ground black pepper
- 5 - fresh mint leaves
- Soda water

INSTRUCTIONS

- Fill a big rocks glass with ice.
- Consolidate the vodka, blackberries, lemon juice, erythritol, dark pepper, and mint leaves in a mixed drink shaker. Tangle until the foods grown from the ground are pounded and have discharged their juices.
- Strain the substance of the mixed drink shaker over best of the ice.
- Top with soft drink water and trimming with blackberries and a new mint leaf.

Nutrition Information: Calories 124g, Fat 9g, Carbs 6g, Sugars 2g, Protein 12g

Low carb tortilla pork rind wraps

Prep Time: 25mins, Cooking Time: 25mins, Servings :1

INGREDIENTS

- 4 - large eggs
- 3 - ounces pork rinds, crushed
- ½ - teaspoon garlic powder
- ¼ - teaspoon ground cumin
- ¼ - ½ - cup water
- Avocado oil or coconut oil, for the pan

INSTRUCTIONS

- In a powerful blender or nourishment processor, consolidate the eggs, red meat skins, garlic powder, and cumin. Mix until easy and all round consolidated. Include a few the water and mix over again. On the off hazard that the blend is extremely thick, preserve on along with water until its miles the consistency of hotcake hitter.
- Warmth an inadequate half teaspoon of oil in an 8-inch nonstick skillet over medium-low warm temperature. Twirl to coat the skillet. Include round 3 tablespoons of the participant and utilize an elastic spatula to spread it meagerly over the base of the skillet, almost to the edges.
- Cook for approximately a second, till the bottom is beginning to darker. Release the edges and carefully flip. Cook the second facet for one greater moment or somewhere within the location.
- Rehash with the rest of the hitter, adding oil to the skillet just as fundamental.
- Add more water to the player as required; it'll thicken as it sits.

Nutrition Information: Calories 168.5g, Fat 12.4g, Carbs 0.9g, Sugars 0.7g, Protein 11.4g

Keto dairy free shamrock shake

Prep Time: 3mins, Cooking Time: 5mins, Servings :1

INGREDIENTS

- ½ - medium avocado
- 1 - scoop dairy free vanilla protein powder (about 30g)
- ½ - cup Silk Almond Coconut Milk
- 8 - ice cubes
- 1/8 - teaspoon peppermint extract
- 5 - drops natural green food coloring
- 2 - tablespoon coconut milk whipped cream
- 1 - tablespoon sugar-free dark chocolate chips

INSTRUCTIONS

- Join the avocado, protein powder, almond coconut milk, ice, peppermint concentrate and sustenance shading in a blender and heartbeat until mixed and rich.
- Top with sans dairy whipped cream and without sugar chocolate chips, if utilizing.

Nutrition Information: Calories 152g, Fat 15g, Carbs 9g, Sugars 1.5g, Protein 4g

Keto honey mustard dressing

Prep Time: 10mins, Cooking Time: 10mins, Servings :2

INGREDIENTS

- ½ - cup full fat sour cream
- ¼ - cup water
- ¼ - cup Dijon mustard
- 1 - tablespoon apple cider vinegar
- 1 - tablespoon granular erythritol

INSTRUCTIONS

- Add all the ingredients in a mixing bowl or container, and mix to form. Keep in the refrigerator up to 2 weeks.

Nutrition Information: Calories 115g, Fat 12g, Carbs 7.5g, Sugars 0.5g, Protein 0.3g

Low carb strawberry margarita gummy

Prep Time: 10mins, Cooking Time: 35mins, Servings :6

INGREDIENTS

- 10 - hulled strawberries, fresh or frozen
- 2 - ounces silver tequila
- 3 - tablespoons grass-fed gelatin collagen protein
- 2 - tablespoons powdered erythritol
- 1 ½ - ounces fresh lime juice

INSTRUCTIONS

- Consolidate the strawberries and tequila in a blender and heartbeat until clean.
- Pour the strawberry-and-tequila blend right into a medium pan and set over low warmth. Include the gelatin, erythritol, and lime squeeze and pace to interrupt up the gelatin and consolidate the fixings.
- Keep on warming for round 10 minutes, whisking each every so often, till the blend ends up pourable. It will begin thick yet will land up greater slender and smoother as it warms.
- Move the mixture to an estimating container or a bowl with a pour gush.
- Rapidly empty the blend into the sticky trojan horse shape and exchange to the fridge.
- Refrigerate for 10 to 15 mins, till set. Pop the sticky worms out of the shape and recognize! Store le overs within the cooler for so long as seven days.

Nutrition Information: Calories 50g, Fat 0.4g, Carbs 2.2g, Sugar 0.4g, Protein 3.2g

Super Easy Spicy Baked Chicken

Prep Time: 25mins, Cooking Time: 45mins, Servings :4

Ingredients

- 4 - ounces cream cheese cut into large chunks
- ½ - cup salsa
- ½ - teaspoon sea salt
- ¼ - teaspoon black pepper freshly ground
- 1 - pound boneless, skinless chicken breasts
- 1 - teaspoon parsley finely chopped, for garnish (optional)

Instructions

- Preheat stove to 350° Fahrenheit.
- Spot cream cheddar and salsa in a little, overwhelming weight pan. Spot over low warmth and cook, blending habitually, until cream cheddar melts and joins with the salsa. Blend in ocean salt and pepper. Expel from warmth. Mastermind chicken bosoms in a heating dish. Pour arranged cream cheddar sauce over best, covering the bosoms.
- Prepare in the preheated stove for 40-45 minutes, or until the focus of chicken bosoms achieve 180° Fahrenheit. Take it off from a stove and sprinkle with parsley, whenever wanted, before serving.

Nutrition Information: Calories 129.5g, Fat 2.2g, Carbs 10.2g, Sugars 2.6g, Protein 18.7g

keto sausage balls

Prep Time: 25mins, Cooking Time: 20mins, Servings :40

INGREDIENTS

- 1 - pound bulk Italian sausage
- 1 - cup blanched almond flour
- 1 - cup shredded sharp cheddar cheese
- ¼ - cup grated Parmesan cheese
- 1 - large egg
- 1 - tablespoon dried minced onions
- 2 - teaspoons baking powder

INSTRUCTIONS

- Preheat the broiler to 350°F. Line a rimmed heating sheet with a wire cooling rack.
- Join the majority of the fixings in a vast blending bowl and, utilizing your hands, blend until very much fused.
- Structure the meat blend into 1/2 – to 2-inch meatballs, making an aggregate of 24
- Spot the meatballs on the wire rack. Heat for 20 minutes or until brilliant dark colored.

Nutrition Information: Calories 170.7g, Fat 16.9g, Carbs 1.8g, Sugars 0.2g, Protein 7g

Pork belly wedge salad

Prep Time: 30mins, Cooking Time: 25mins, Servings :4

INGREDIENTS

- 1 - large head iceberg lettuce, quartered
- 1 - cup Creamy Chive Blue Cheese Dressing.
- 12 - ounces pork belly, cooked crisp and chopped
- 12 - grape tomatoes, halved
- 2 - tablespoons chopped red onion
- ¼ - cup blue cheese crumbles
- A -few sprigs fresh dill weed
- 2 - tablespoons Everything Bagel Seasoning

INSTRUCTIONS

- Set each iceberg wedge on a salad plate, pinnacle with blue cheese dressing, or desired dressing of choice
- After which divide the relaxation of the toppings similarly among all 4 wedges.

Nutrition Information: Calories 250.8g, Fat 21g, Carbs 5.9g, Sugars 3.1g, Protein 10.9g

Pickled red onions

Prep Time: 45mins, Cooking Time: 30mins, Servings :8

INGREDIENTS

- 1 - cup red wine vinegar
- 1 - cup apple cider vinegar
- 2 - tablespoons granular erythritol, more to taste
- 1 - teaspoons sea salt
- 2 - medium red onions, thinly sliced
- 6 - cloves garlic, peeled and halved
- 1 - teaspoon dried oregano leaves
- Pinch of red pepper flakes

INSTRUCTIONS

- In a pan over medium warm temperature, be a part of the red wine vinegar, apple juice vinegar, erythritol, and salt. Convey to a mild bubble, blending until the erythritol and salt are damaged down.
- Put the onions, garlic, oregano, and purple pepper portions into a 32-ounce bricklayer field.
- Pour the fluid over satisfactory, submerging the onions and mixing inside the oregano and red pepper chips.
- Give the box a danger to sit on the counter for 60 minutes, pinnacle and afterward refrigerate
- save inside the fridge for as long as 2 months. you could devour them following 2 hours, however they absolutely show signs and symptoms of development and higher the more they may be within the cooler.

Nutrition Information: Calories 59.1g, Fat 0.2g, Carbs 16g, Sugars 14.7g, Protein 0.2g

Everything but the bagel seasoning

Prep Time: 35mins, Cooking Time: 40mins, Servings :5

INGREDIENTS

- ¼ - cup toasted sesame seeds
- 3 - tablespoons, plus
- 1 - teaspoon poppy seeds
- 3 - tablespoons, plus
- 1 - teaspoon dried minced onions
- 3 - tablespoons, plus
- 1 - teaspoon dried garlic flakes
- 2 - tablespoons coarse sea salt

INSTRUCTIONS

- Add all the ingredients together for mixing and store in an airtight container. Shake before using.

Nutrition Information: Calories 61g, Fat 1.5g, Carbs 3.5g, Sugar 0.9g, Protein 0.8g

Crispy baked garlic parmesan wings

Prep Time: 35mins, Cooking Time: 1hr 20mins, Servings :8

INGREDIENTS

- 2 - pounds pork baby back ribs
- 2 - tablespoons olive oil
- 1 - batch Barbecue Dry Rub

- INSTRUCTIONS
- Preheat the oven to 300°f. Line a rimmed baking sheet with aluminum foil.
- Cast off the skinny membrane from the back, or concave aspect, of the ribs. Begin through reducing into the membrane with a pointy knife, and then pull the skin away from the ribs. Set the ribs at the coated baking sheet.
- Brush the olive oil lightly over the ribs. Pour the dry rub over the ribs and paintings it lightly onto both sides.
- Bake until the ribs are soft and juicy at the internal and fine and crispy at the out of doors, about 2 half of hours. Shop leftovers within the refrigerator for up to 1 week.

Nutrition Information: Calories 261g, Fat 23.2g, Carbs 1.5g, Sugar 1.5g, Protein 11.6g

Pumpkin spice roasted pecans

Prep Time: 25mins, Cooking Time: 40mins, Servings :6

INGREDIENTS

- 2 - cups raw pecan
- 3 - tablespoons salted butter, melted
- 1 - teaspoon pure vanilla extract
- 2 - tablespoons Pumpkin Pie Spice
- 2 - tablespoons confectioners erythritol

INSTRUCTIONS

- Preheat the broiler to 350°F. Line a rimmed preparing sheet with a silicone heating mat or material paper.
- Include the pecans, margarine and vanilla to a blending bowl. Utilize an elastic spatula to hurl the nuts and coat them uniformly in the softened margarine.
- Sprinkle the pumpkin pie flavor and erythritol over best. Hurl to blend in and equally coat the nuts.
- Spread the nuts over the heating sheet in a solitary layer.
- Heat for 12 minutes.

Nutrition Information: Calories 114.4g, Fat 9.7g, Carbs 7.2g, Sugars 5.5g, Protein 1.5g

Low carb keto banana nut protein pancakes

Prep Time: 35mins, Cooking Time: 45mins, Servings:3

INGREDIENTS

- 2 - scoops Banana Nut Protein Powder (56 grams)
- 2 - ounces cream cheese, softened
- 4 - large pastured eggs
- 1 - teaspoon pure vanilla extract
- 2 - teaspoons baking powder
- 1 - tablespoon confectioners erythritol
- Butter for cooking

INSTRUCTIONS

- Consolidate all fixings in a high powder blender. Heartbeat till all fixings is clean and all round joined. You may additionally want to massage the perimeters with an elastic spatula and heartbeat again to ensure the entirety is totally combined.
- Brush a enormous non-stick skillet or frying pan field with unfold and heat over medium-low warmth. When the dish is warm, include 1/4 measure of the hitter and cook till it's far bubbly to finish everything and fantastic darker on the base, round 3 minutes. Flip and prepare dinner the alternative aspect until it is amazing darkish colored, round 2-3mins. Rehash this process till all the player is no more.

Nutrition Information: Calories 149.5g, Fat 13.3g, Carbs 4g, Sugars 0.7g, Protein 6.1g

5 Minute Low Carb Chicken Nuggets

Prep Time: 25mins, Cooking Time: 20mins, Servings :6

Ingredients

- 2 - cups cooked chicken
- 8 - oz cream cheese, 1 - egg
- ¼ - cup almond flour, 1 - tsp garlic salt

Instructions

- Shred chicken with an electric blender. This works high-quality with a mix of dim and chicken (or truly dull meat) that is still heat.
- On the off danger which you are using remaining bird warm it up rather first. When the hen is destroyed encompass something is left of the fixings and mix till completely consolidated.
- Drop scoops onto a lubed heating sheet (or use cloth paper to line it) and clean into a bit form.
- Prepare at 350 for 12-14 min till fairly exquisite and firm.

Nutrition Information: Calories 187.5g, Fat 2.6g, Carbs 12.6g, Sugars 1.6g, Protein 27.3g

Sausage Kale Soup with Mushroom

Prep Time: 35mins, Cooking Time: 40mins, Servings :6

Ingredients

- 29 - ounces chicken bone broth
- 6.5 - ounces fresh kale cut into bite sized pieces
- 1 - pound sausage cooked, casings removed and sliced
- 6.5 - ounces sliced mushrooms
- 2 - cloves garlic minced
- Salt & Pepper to taste

Instructions

- Spot the two jars of chicken soup in expansive pot alongside two jars worth of water. Heat to the point of boiling over medium warmth.
- Include the kale, wiener, mushrooms and garlic. Season to taste with salt and pepper.
- Stew secured over low warmth for around 60 minutes.

Nutrition Information: Calories 350.2g, Fat 8.1g, Carbs 51.8g, Sugars 8g, Protein 20g

White Lasagna Stuffed Peppers

Prep Time: 35mins, Cooking Time: 45mins, Servings :4

Ingredients

- 2 - large sweet peppers halved and seeded
- 1 - tsp garlic salt divided
- 12 - oz ground turkey
- ¾ - cup ricotta cheese
- 1 - cup mozzarella
- 8 - cherry tomatoes

Instructions

- Preheat stove to 400.
- Put the split peppers in a preparing dish. Sprinkle with 1/4 tsp garlic salt. Partition the ground turkey between the peppers and press into the bottoms. Sprinkle with another 1/4 tsp garlic salt. Heat for 30 minutes.
- Gap the ricotta cheddar between the peppers. Sprinkle with the rest of the 1/2 tsp garlic salt. Sprinkle the mozzarella to finish everything. Put the cherry tomatoes in the middle of the peppers, if utilizing.
- Prepare for an extra 30 minutes until the peppers are mollified, the meat is cooked, and the cheddar is brilliant.

Nutrition Information: Calories 112.8g, Fat 1.4g, Carbs 22.5g, Sugars 4.8g, Protein 7.9g

Creamy Basil Baked Sausage

Prep Time: 20mins, Cooking Time: 40mins, Servings :4

Ingredients

- 3 - lb Italian sausage chicken, turkey, or pork
- 8 - oz cream cheese
- ¼ - cup basil pesto
- ¼ - cup heavy cream
- 8 - oz mozzarella

Instructions

- Preheat broiler to 400. Shower a huge meal dish with the cooking splash. Put the frankfurter in the heating dish. Prepare for 30 minutes.
- In the mean time blend together the cream cheddar, pesto, and overwhelming cream.
- Spread the sauce over the frankfurter. Top with mozzarella. Prepare for an extra 10 minutes or until the hotdog is 160 degrees when checked with a meat thermometer.

Nutrition Information: Calories 336.7g, Fat 15.3g, Carbs 25g, Sugars 1.3g, Protein 33g

Easy Taco Casserole Recipe

Prep Time: 25mins, Cooking Time: 40mins, Servings :4

Ingredients

- 1.5 to 2 - lb ground turkey or beef
- 2 - tbsp taco seasoning
- 1 - cup salsa
- 16 - oz cottage cheese
- 8 - oz shredded cheddar cheese

Instructions

- Preheat stove to 400.
- Blend the ground meat and taco flavoring in a huge meal dish. Mine is 11 x 13. Prepare for 20 minutes.
- In the interim, combine the curds, salsa, and 1 measure of the cheddar. Put aside.
- Take off the meal dish from the stove and cautiously channel the cooling fluid from the meat. Separate the meat into little pieces. A potato masher works incredible for this. Spread the curds and salsa blend over the meat. Sprinkle the rest of the cheddar to finish everything.
- Return the meal to the stove and heat for an extra 15-20 minutes until the meat is cooked completely and the cheddar is hot and bubbly.

Nutrition Information: Calories 281.9g, Fat 14.2g, Carbs 21.4g, Sugars 1.5g, Protein 16.7g

Stuffed Pork Chops - 5 Ingredients

Prep Time: 20mins, Cooking Time: 35mins, Servings :8

Ingredients

- 12 - thin cut boneless pork chops , about 2 - 2.5 pounds
- 4 - garlic cloves, 1 ½ - tsp salt
- 2 - cups baby spinach , about 2.5 oz
- 12 - slices provolone cheese (about 8 oz)

Instructions

- Preheat the range to 350.
- Press the garlic cloves via a garlic press into a touch bowl. Add the salt and mix to consolidate. Spread the garlic rub on one aspect of the beef hacks.
- Slashes garlic aspect down onto an expansive rimmed heating sheet. Gap the spinach between the ones 6 cleaves. Crease the cheddar cuts down the center and placed them over the spinach. Put second pork lower over each with the garlic facet up.
- Heat for 20mins. Spread each pork cleave with another cut of cheddar. Back for a further 10-15mins or till the meat is a hundred and sixty stages whilst checked with a meat thermometer.

Nutrition Information: Calories 240.5g, Fat 10.7g, Carbs 8.7g, Sugars 0.5g, Protein 25.9g

Chocolate peanut butter no bake cookies

Prep Time: 35mins, Cooking Time: 40mins, Servings:2

INGREDIENTS

- ¼ - cup creamy thick natural peanut butter
- ¼ - cup creamy thick natural almond butter
- 3 - tablespoons cream cheese, softened
- 2 - tablespoons salted butter, melted
- 1 - teaspoon pure vanilla extract
- 2 - tablespoons unsweetened cocoa powder
- 2 - tablespoons confectioners erythritol, more to taste
- ¾ - cup unsweetened desiccated coconut

INSTRUCTIONS

- Set a preparing sheet with a silicone heating mat.
- In a mixing bowl, consolidate the nutty unfold, almond margarine, and creamy cheddar. Blend till easy.
- Include the spread, vanilla listens, and cocoa powder. What's greater, erythritol. Blend until all fixings are very tons joined.
- Utilizing an elastic spatula overlay inside the coconut. Blend until it's far equitably disseminated during the blend.
- Drop half to 2-inch spoonfuls (10 absolute) onto the readied heating sheet.
- Stop for 10mins earlier than serving.
- Store extra items inside the cooler until prepared to eat.

Nutrition Information: Calories 105.9g, Fat 3.7g, Carbs 17.2g, Sugars 12.1g, Protein 1.9g

Low carb keto nut free pizza crust

Prep Time: 25mins, Cooking Time: 45mins, Servings:8

INGREDIENTS

- 4 - oz cream cheese, softened
- 2 - large eggs
- ½ - tsp garlic powder
- ½ - tsp onion powder
- ½ - tsp dried Italian seasoning
- ¼ - cup grated parmesan cheese
- 1 ¼ - cup shredded mozzarella cheese

INSTRUCTIONS

- Preheat the broiler to 375°F Line a 12-inch pizza skillet with fabric paper. Then again you can do that on a getting ready dish, fixed with cloth paper or a silicone heating mat, or even in a lined meal dish. Work with what you've got.
- In a blending bowl, using a hand blender, consolidate eggs, creamy cheddar, and flavoring. There will be some little clusters, but it ought to be generally clean.
- Utilizing an elastic spatula, crease in the parmesan and mozzarella cheeses.
- Move combo to the lined pizza box. Spread the blend out in a flimsy, even circle. For a thicker masking, make a little circle.
- Prepare for 22mins, flipping 12-14 minutes in. To turn it without breaking it, I like to pinnacle it with the second little bit of material paper and lift it up from the bottom, flipping it over with the brand new sheet of fabric paper under the outside, over the pizza field.

Nutrition Information: Calories 147g, Fat 10g, Carbs 4g, Sugars 1g, Protein 14g

LOW CARB TURKEY CLUB PINWHEELS

Prep Time: 25mins, Cooking Time: 30mins, Servings:20

INGREDIENTS

- 2 - Large Low Carb Tortillas
- 12 - Slices Deli Turkey
- 6 - Strips Thick Cut Bacon – Cooked Crisp
- 4 - oz. Roasted Red Peppers
- 2 - oz. Cream Cheese – Softened
- 2 - Tbs. Ranch Dressing
- 1 - Medium Avocado – Peeled, Pitted and Sliced

Instructions

- Join cream cheddar and farm dressing and separation similarly between the two tortillas. Spread equitably, covering one entire side of every tortilla.
- Top every tortilla with half of the turkey, bacon, broiled red peppers, and avocado cuts.
- Move up firmly, being mindful so as not to press the fixings out of the sides.
- Wrap firmly in cling wrap and refrigerate for 30 minutes or until the wraps are firm enough to cut

Nutrition Information: Calories 206.9g, Fat 8.9g, Carbs 20.9g, Sugars 0.4g, Protein 9g

Caprese snack

Prep Time: 25mins, Cooking Time: 35mins, Servings:12

Ingredients

- 8 - oz. cherry tomatoes
- 8 - oz. mozzarella, mini cheese balls
- 2 - tbsp green pesto
- salt and pepper

Instructions

- Cut the tomatoes and mozzarella balls fifty-fifty. Include pesto and blend.
- Salt and pepper to taste.

Nutrition Information: Calories 140.9g, Fat 9.5g, Carbs 4.2g, Sugars 1.3g, Protein 9.5g

Oriental red cabbage salad

Prep Time: 25mins, Cooking Time: 25mins, Servings:4

Ingredients

- 30 - oz. red cabbage
- 4¼ - oz. butter
- 1 - tsp salt
- ¼ - tsp ground black pepper
- 1 - cinnamon stick
- 1 - tbsp red wine vinegar
- 1 - orange, juice and zest
- 2 - tbsp fresh dill, chopped

Instructions

- Shred the cabbage finely, in a perfect world with a mandolin slicer or in a nourishment processor.
- Broil in a spread on medium high for 10– 15 minutes. Sear the cabbage delicately until delicate and sparkly - not very dark colored.
- Salt and pepper. Include cinnamon, vinegar and squeezed the orange. Let stew for 5-10 minutes.
- Include pizzazz and dill towards the end or when serving.

Nutrition Information: Calories 64.3g, Fat 3.6g, Carbs 8.7g, Sugars 6.5g, Protein 0.8g

Salad in a jar

Prep Time: 15mins, Cooking Time: 10mins, Servings:4

Ingredients

- 4 - oz. smoked salmon or rotisserie chickens
- 1/6 - oz. leafy greens
- 1/6 - oz. cherry tomatoes
- 1/6 - oz. red bell peppers
- 1/6 - oz. cucumber
- ½ - scallion
- 4 - tbsp mayonnaise or olive oil

Instructions

- Shred or hack vegetables of your decision. In the first place, put dim verdant greens, for example, spinach or arugula at the base of the container. Ice shelf lettuce or romaine works as well. Green and red cabbage gives a crisp crunch. Hacked broccoli or cauliflower additionally works extraordinarily.
- Include cut onion rings, destroyed carrot, avocado, distinctive ringer peppers and tomato in layers.
- We have finished our serving of mixed greens with smoked salmon and barbecued chicken, yet you can obviously utilize your very own most loved protein, bubbled eggs, mackerel or canned fish or any sort of virus cuts you need. Olives, nuts, seeds, and cheddar 3D squares are extraordinary tasty increments.
- To feel fulfilled, you might need to include a liberal measure of dressing or mayonnaise that you store in a different little container or jug and include directly before serving.

Nutrition Information: Calories 293.3g, Fat 16.9g, Carbs 10.1g, Sugars 0.5, Protein 27.3g

Coleslaw

Prep Time: 20mins, Cooking Time: 10mins, Servings:8

Ingredients

- ½ - lb green cabbage
- ½ - lemon, the juice
- 1 - tsp salt
- ½ - cup mayonnaise
- 1 - pinch fennel seeds (optional)
- 1 - pinch pepper
- 1 - tbsp Dijon mustard

Instructions

- Take off the center and shred the cabbage utilizing a nourishment processor, mandolin or sharp cheddar slicer.
- Spot the cabbage in a medium-sized bowl.
- Include salt and lemon juice.
- Mix and permit take a seat for 10mins to offer the cabbage a chance to reduce rather. Dispose of any abundance of fluid.
- Blend cabbage, mayonnaise, and discretionary mustard.
- Season to taste.

Nutrition Information: Calories 71.7g, Fat 4.5g, Carbs 7.9g, Sugars 1.8g, Protein 0.8g

Asian Lobster Salad

Prep Time: 25mins, Cooking Time: 30mins, Servings:4

NGREDIENTS

- ¾ - lb Northern Lobster
- 2 - cup, shreddeds Chinese Cabbage (Bok-Choy, Pak-Choi)
- ½ - small Sweet Red Pepper
- 4 - medium (4-1/8" long) Scallions or Spring Onions
- 1 - tbsp Dried Whole Sesame Seeds
- 2 - tbsps Sodium and Sugar Free Rice Vinegar
- 2 - tbsps Tamari Soybean Sauce, 1 - tsp Ginger
- 1 - tbsp Canola Vegetable Oil, 1 - tsp Sesame Oil

Instructions

- For the plate of mixed greens: In an expansive serving bowl, join lobster, cabbage, ringer pepper, scallions, and sesame seeds.
- For the dressing: In a little bowl, whisk the rice vinegar, Tamari soy sauce, ground ginger, and the canola and sesame oils together.
- Pour dressing over the serving of mixed greens and hurl delicately to coat. Season with crisp ground dark pepper and salt.

Nutrition Information: Calories 159.2g, Fat 2.5g, Carbs 2.8g, Sugars 0.2g, Protein 29.5g

Sian-Style Coleslaw

Prep Time: 20mins, Cooking Time: 25mins, Servings:6

INGREDIENTS

- 1 - cup, chopped Snowpeas (Pea Pod)
- 1 - large (7-1/4" to 8-1/2" long) Carrots
- 12 - oz Chinese Cabbage (Bok-Choy, Pak-Choi)
- 2 - tablespoons Extra Virgin Olive Oil
- 1 - tbsp Toasted Sesame Oil
- 2 - tbsps Sodium and Sugar Free Rice Vinegar
- 1 - tbsp Tamari Soybean Sauce
- 2 - tsps Ginger
- 1 - tsp No Calorie Sweetener

Instructions

- Shredd cabbage at that point place in a vast bowl. Mesh the carrot into a cabbage. Blend in daintily cut snow peas.
- In a little bowl, blend oils, vinegar, tamari, ginger, and sugar substitute.
- Pour dressing over a plate of mixed greens; hurl to coat. Season to taste with salt.

Nutrition Information: Calories 226g, Fat 18.5g, Carbs 12.5g, Sugars 6.6g, Protein 3g

Roast Beef Red Bell Pepper

Prep Time: 35mins, Cooking Time: 25mins, Servings:6

INGREDIENTS

- 2 - inner leaves Romaine Lettuce
- 1 - tbsp Real Mayonnaise
- ½ - tsp Horseradish
- 2 - oz Provolone Cheese
- 4 - oz boneless, cooked Roast Beef
- ¼ - medium Red Sweet Pepper

INSTRUCTIONS

- Evacuate base segment of lettuce leaves. Lay level on a spotless surface. Top each with a cut of cheddar.
- Join the mayonnaise with horseradish including garlic powder and season with salt and crisply ground dark pepper.
- Spread onto cheddar cuts. At that point place a layer of meal hamburger.
- Cut the red ringer pepper into 1/4-inch thick strips and lay toward one side of the meal meat, cheddar and lettuce.
- Move up, beginning where you set the pepper strips until completely rolled. Secure with a tooth pick, rehash for second move up and appreciate right away.

Nutrition Information: Calories 381.9g, Fat 23.2g, Carbs 6.9g, Sugars 2.3g, Protein 35.4g

Bacon-Egg Salad Flatout Wrap

Prep Time: 20mins, Cooking Time: 15mins, Servings:4

INGREDIENTS

- 2 - large Boiled Eggs
- 1 - tbsp Real Mayonnaise
- ½ - tsp or 1 packet Yellow Mustard
- 1 - flatbread Light Original Flatbread
- 1 ½ - oz, cookeds Turkey Bacon
- 1 - inner leaf Romaine Lettuce

INSTRUCTIONS

- Combine cleaved eggs, mayonnaise, and mustard. Add salt and pepper to taste.
- Spread blend on one adjusted end of Flat-out that has the lettuce smoothed out on it.
- Top with cooked broke bacon at that point move up and cut down the middle.

Nutrition Information: Calories 429.8g, Fat 30.6g, Carbs 10.2g, Sugars 0.7g, Protein 31.3g

Buffalo Chicken Salad

Prep Time: 35mins, Cooking Time: 30mins, Servings:4

INGREDIENTS

- ½ - fruit Lemon
- 1 - medium Young Green Onions
- 1 - head Cos or Romaine Lettuce
- 2 - stalk, medium Celery
- 1 - medium Red Sweet Pepper
- 1 - medium Tomato
- 1 - large Egg
- 5 1/3 – tbsp. Apple Cider Vinegar
- 1/8 - tsp Celery Salt
- 1/8 - tsp Red or Cayenne Pepper
- 2 - Chicken Thigh Meat and Skin
- ¼ - cup Real Mayonnaise
- 2 - tbsp Sour Cream
- 2/3 - oz Blue Cheese
- 1/8 - tsp Garlic Powder
- 1/3 - tsp Salt
- ¼ - tsp Black Pepper

INSTRUCTIONS

- Juice the lemon into an intensive bowl casting off any seeds.
- Finely cleave the inexperienced onions and add to the bowl; placed aside.
- To the bowl with the lemon squeeze and green onions, encompass the mayonnaise, sharp cream, cheddar, and garlic powder and mix to enroll in.

- Evacuate the stem, essence, and seeds from the purple ringer pepper and remove.
- Cut the ringer pepper into¼-inch slender strips.
- Utilizing a fork beat the egg in some other medium bowl. Include the apple juice vinegar, ¼ box canola oil, ¼ teaspoon of dark pepper, a ⅓ teaspoon of salt
- Pat the bird thighs with paper towels and add to the marinade, at that factor region on a sheet container fixed with foil.
- Prepare for 18 to twenty minutes, turning the thighs and combing with the marinade a few instances, until cooked via and sparkling.
- Cut the bird thighs into ½-inch diced portions and put aside for level 6.
- Expel the plate of blended greens from the icebox and hurl to sign up for.
- Separation the serving of veggies among to plates and spot the bird in the interior.

Nutrition Information: Calories 384g, Fat 19g, Carbs 15g, Sugars 0.3g, Protein 43g

Cheese Straws

Prep Time: 25mins, Cooking Time: 55mins, Servings:4

INGREDIENTS

- 6 - tablespoons Unsalted Butter Stick
- ½ - tsp Garlic Powder
- ¾ - cup, shredded Cheddar Cheese
- ¼ - cup Parmesan Cheese
- 2 - large Eggs
- ½ - serving Garlic Salt
- 3 - servings Atkins Flour Mix

INSTRUCTIONS

- Utilize the Atkins formula to make Atkins Flour Mix for this formula.
- Preheat broiler to 375°F.
- Spot heating blend, spread, and garlic powder in a nourishment processor. Procedure until blend looks like coarse scraps.
- Include cheeses and eggs. Heartbeat just until mixture meets up.
- Exchange batter onto an expansive bit of cling wrap. Softly structure into a level round. Place the second bit of fold around mixture.
- Press or move batter to a 6 x 12 square shape, around 1/2 thick. Refrigerate until exceptionally firm, somewhere around 2 hours.
- Spot mixture on a level plane on the ledge. Expel top sheet of plastic from the batter. Sprinkle with garlic salt; delicately press into mixture.
- With a sharp blade cut mixture into forty 6-inch long strips. Transfer strips to an ungreased heating sheet.

- Prepare 12-15 minutes, until delicately cooked. Slide straws onto a cooling rack. Whenever cool, store in a hermetically sealed holder. 3 stick equivalents one serving.

Nutrition Information: Calories 47.1g, Fat 3.2g, Carbs 2.6g, Sugars 0.5g, Protein 1.9g

Ham, Cream Cheese and Pickle Roll-Ups | Atkins

Prep Time: 25mins, Cooking Time: 40mins, Servings:4

INGREDIENTS

- 2 - oz boneless, cooked Fresh Ham
- 2 - tbsp Cream Cheese
- 2 - spears Pickles

INSTRUCTIONS

- Spread 1 tablespoon cream cheddar on each cut of ham.
- Spot a pickle stick toward one side of each ham cut and move up.
- Secure with a tooth pick whenever wanted.

Nutrition Information: Calories 24.7g, Fat 1.4g, Carbs 1.8g, Sugars 0.3g, Protein 1.2g

Garlic Ranch Dressing

Prep Time: 35mins, Cooking Time: 45mins, Servings:2

INGREDIENTS

- ¾ - cup Real Mayonnaise
- ½ - cup Buttermilk (Reduced Fat, Cultured)
- ¾ - tsp Onion Powder
- 2 - tbsp Parsley
- ½ - tsp Garlic
- 1 - tsp Dijon Mustard
- 1/8 - tsp Salt
- 1/8 - tsp Black Pepper
- 1 - tsp Fresh Lemon Juice

INSTRUCTIONS

- Join all fixings in a blender; puree until smooth.
- Season to taste with salt and crisply ground dark pepper.

Nutrition Information: Calories 91.6g, Fat 9.2g, Carbs 1.6g, Sugars 1.1g, Protein 0.8g

Crab and Avocado Salad

Prep Time: 45mins, Cooking Time: 40mins, Servings:4

INGREDIENTS

- 3 - tbsp Real Mayonnaise, 2 - tbsp Fresh Lime Juice
- 1 - tsp Cumin, ½ - tsp Paprika, 16 - oz Canned Crab
- 2 - stalk, medium Celery
- 1 - fruit without skin and seed California Avocado
- 3 - cup Watercress

INSTRUCTIONS

- In a huge bowl, blend mayonnaise, lime juice, cumin, and paprika.
- Include crab meat and diced celery. Blend well; include salt and newly ground dark pepper to taste.
- 3D squares the avocado and tenderly blends it into the blend.
- On the other hand, this plate of mixed greens looks extraordinary served in the well of avocado parts as opposed to cubing the avocado essentially evacuates the seed and the skin.
- Gap watercress on four plates; top with serving of mixed greens.

Nutrition Information: Calories 46.6g, Fat 3.1g, Carbs 1.6g, Sugars 1.3g, Protein 2.6g

Sausage Kale Soup with Mushroom

Prep Time: 35mins, Cooking Time: 60mins, Servings:6

Ingredients

- 29 - ounces chicken bone broth
- 6.5 - ounces fresh kale cut into bite sized pieces
- 1 - pound sausage cooked, casings removed and sliced
- 6.5 - ounces sliced mushrooms
- 2 - cloves garlic minced
- Salt & Pepper to taste

Instructions

- Spot the two jars of chicken soup in expansive pot alongside two jars worth of water. Heat to the point of boiling over medium warmth.
- Include the kale, wiener, mushrooms and garlic. Season to taste with salt and pepper.
- Stew secured over low warmth for around 60 minutes.

Nutrition Information: Calories 262.5g, Fat 16.1g, Carbs 17g, Sugars 4.2g, Protein 14.9g

PARMESAN CHICKEN TENDERS

Prep Time: 25mins, Cooking Time: 35mins, Servings: 4

INGREDIENTS

- 1 2.5 - lb. bag chicken tenderloins
- ¾ - cup butter
- 1⅛ - cup parmesan cheese
- ¾ - tsp. garlic powder, Salt, to taste

INSTRUCTIONS

- Soften the margarine in a skillet and include the parmesan cheddar and garlic powder (and salt, if utilizing). Plunge the chicken in the blend and spot on a treat sheet. Prepare at 325 degrees F for 20-30 minutes (until the chicken is never again pink inside and the juices run clear). Don't overbake!
- We have likewise utilized these for Sunday lunch. My mother set them up for chapel, at that point heated them on our stove's "warm" setting for about 3½ hours while we were no more. Worked incredible!

Nutrition Information: Calories 306g, Fat 8.6g, Carbs 9.8g, Sugars 1g, Protein 27.7g

Chicken al Forno & Vodka Sauce with Two Cheeses

Prep Time: 25mins, Cooking Time: 30mins, Servings: 6

Ingredients

- 2 - pounds chicken breast (cooked and cut into chunks)
- 1 ½ - cups vodka sauce jarred or homemade
- ½ - cup parmesan cheese
- 16 - oz fresh mozzarella
- fresh spinach optional

Instructions

- Preheat the broiler to 400. Splash a meal dish with cooking shower. Include the cooked chicken.
- Top with the vodka sauce, parmesan cheddar, and lumps of new mozzarella.
- Heat until hot and bubbly. Around 25-30 minutes.
- Discretionary: You can serve this over child spinach. The warmth from the sauce shrinks the spinach.

Nutrition Information: Calories 347g, Fat 16g, Carbs 38.2g, Sugars 0.3g, Protein 13.2g

Lemon Parmesan Broccoli Soup

Prep Time: 35mins, Cooking Time: 40mins, Servings: 4-6

Ingredients

- 2.5 to 3 - lbs of fresh broccoli florets
- 4 - cups of water
- 2 - cups unsweetened almond milk
- ¾ - cup parmesan cheese
- 2 - tbsp lemon juice

Instructions

- Put the broccoli and water in a substantial pan. Spread and cook on medium high until the broccoli is delicate.
- Save one measure of the cooling fluid and dispose of the rest.
- Include half of the broccoli, the saved cooking fluid, and almond milk into a blender. Mix until smooth.
- Come back to the pot with whatever is left of the broccoli. Include the parmesan and lemon squeeze and warmth until hot.
- I didn't include salt or pepper however you might need to include a bit. Simply season to taste.

Nutrition Information: Calories 181.6g, Fat 7.6g, Carbs 18.2g, Sugars 0.7g, Protein 11g

Fresh Tomato Basil Soup

Prep Time: 30mins, Cooking Time: 30mins, Servings: 6

Ingredients

- 5 - cups of fresh tomato puree
- 1 - stick of salted butter
- 8 - oz cream cheese
- a - handful of fresh basil leaves
- 1 - tbsp Trim Healthy Mama Gentle Sweet
- salt and pepper to taste

Instructions

- Puree enough new tomatoes in a blender to measure up to five measures of puree. This was around 4 extensive tomatoes and perhaps a half quart of cherry tomatoes.
- Turn the puree into a substantial pan and include the spread and creamy cheddar. Warmth to a stew and cook until the margarine and cream cheddar liquefy. Cautiously empty the soup once more into the blender and include the basil (use alert mixing hot fluids - dependably vent the top) or utilize a drenching blender to puree until smooth.

Nutrition Information: Calories 210g, Fat 10g, Carbs 11g, Sugars 0.5g, Protein 12g

Ranch Yogurt Marinade for Grilled Chicken

Prep Time: 40mins, Cooking Time: 2hrs 20mins, Servings: 4

Ingredients

- 1/3 - cup plain yogurt
- 1 - tbsp dill
- 1 - tbsp parsley
- 1 - tbsp onion powder
- 1 - tbsp garlic powder
- 1 - tsp salt

Instructions

- Mix all ingredients in a single bowl. Add 2.5 lbs of the chicken tenders. Marinade in the fridge for at least 4 hours.

Nutrition Information: Calories 41g, Fat 0.3g, Carbs 4.5g, Sugars 1.9g, Protein 4.7g

Keto sausage and egg breakfast sandwich

Prep Time: 35mins, Cooking Time: 40mins, Servings: 1-2

INGREDIENTS

- 1 - tbsp butter
- 2 - large eggs
- 1 - tbsp mayonnaise
- 2 - sausage patties, cooked
- 2 - slices sharp cheddar cheese
- a - few slices of avocado

INSTRUCTIONS

- Warmth the margarine in a huge skillet over medium warmth. Spot delicately oiled artisan container rings or silicone egg molds into the dish.
- Split the eggs into the rings and utilize a fork to break the yolks and tenderly whisk. Spread and cook for 3-4 minutes or until eggs are cooked through. Take off the eggs from the rings.
- Spot one of the eggs on a plate and best it with half of the mayonnaise. Top the egg with one of the wiener patties.

Nutrition Information: Calories 178.5g, Fat 1.9g, Carbs 9.1g, Sugars 0.4g, Protein 28.3g

Hot crab and artichoke dip

Prep Time: 20mins, Cooking Time: 35mins, Servings: 10

INGREDIENTS

- 8 - oz lump crab meat
- 14 - oz can artichoke hearts, drained and chopped
- 1 - cup sharp cheddar cheese, shredded
- ¾ - cup Parmesan cheese, shredded, divided
- ¾ - cup sour cream, ½ - cup mayonnaise
- 3 - green onions, chopped
- 3 - large cloves garlic, minced
- 1 - tsp garlic powder, 1 - tsp onion powder

INSTRUCTIONS

- Preheat stove to 350°
- In an extensive blending bowl, join crab meat, artichoke hearts, cheddar, ½ container Parmesan cheddar, acrid cream, mayonnaise, green onion, garlic, garlic powder, and onion powder. Blend until all fixings are all around fused.
- Move crab blend into a shallow preparing dish.
- Prepare for 30 minutes on top rack.
- Sprinkle remaining ¼ container Parmesan cheddar over the best and sear on high 3-5 minutes.

Nutrition Information: Calories 195.9g, Fat 5.2g, Carbs 9g, Sugars 2g, Protein 28.7g

Roasted red pepper garlic aioli

Prep Time: 25mins, Cooking Time: 30mins, Servings: 6

INGREDIENTS

- ¾ - cup mayo
- 6 - cloves garlic, minced
- 2 - tablespoons fresh lemon juice
- ½ - cup chopped roasted red peppers
- a - few sprigs fresh flat-leaf parsley
- ¼ - teaspoon sea salt, more to taste
- pinch of black pepper, more to taste

INSTRUCTIONS

- Place all substances in a food processor or excessive-powered blender and pulse till well blended and smooth.
- Refrigerate for as a minimum 30 minutes before serving.

Nutrition Information: Calories 33.1g, Fat 2g, Carbs 3.8g, Sugars 1.8g, Protein 0.3g

Easy Low Carb Breakfast Casserole

Prep Time: 30mins, Cooking Time: 48mins, Servings: 6

Ingredients

- 1 - pound Ground breakfast sausage
- 1 - tablespoon Garlic minced
- 2 - cups Bell peppers diced
- ½ - cup Yellow onion diced
- 3 - cups Spinach chopped, 12 - Eggs
- 1/8 - teaspoon each Salt and pepper or to taste
- ½ - cup Cheddar cheese shredded

Instructions

- Preheat broiler to 350 degrees F and set up a preparing dish with non-stick cooking shower and put aside.
- Ground and cook wiener in a skillet until completely cooked. Include garlic, peppers, and onions to the skillet and sauté with a hotdog for 2 minutes. Spot this in your readied heating dish. Include cleaved spinach top.
- In a different bowl whisk eggs with salt and pepper. Pour egg wash over vegetables in the heating dish and tenderly blend to ensure eggs are covering the whole dish. Top with cheddar and prepare for 45 minutes or until a fork can tell the truth and eggs are cooked entirely through.

Nutrition Information: Calories 223.6g, Fat 15.4g, Carbs 7.6g, Sugars 0.7g, Protein 13.2g

Asparagus and Leek Soup

Prep Time: 20mins, Cooking Time: 18mins, Servings: 4

INGREDIENTS

- 2 - tablespoons Unsalted Butter Stick
- 1 - each Leeks, ¾ - lb Asparagus, 1 - tsp Garlic
- 1 14.5 - oz can Chicken Broth, Bouillon or Consomme
- 1/3 - cup Heavy Cream

Instructions

- Liquefy margarine in an extensive pot over medium-high warmth. Clean the leeks and bones the white and a portion of the green tops. Hack asparagus into 1-2 inch pieces.
- Add to leeks to the container and sauté for 3 minutes. Include asparagus and cook 1 minute more. Include garlic and sauté for 30 additional seconds.
- Add stock to pot and heat to the point of boiling.
- Lower warmth, spread and stew 8 to 10 minutes, until asparagus is delicate.
- Blend in cream, and season with salt and naturally ground dark pepper. Mix soup in a nourishment processor or blender until smooth.
- Come back to pot to warm through before serving (if important). Season with extra salt and newly ground dark pepper to taste.

Nutrition Information: Calories 93.9g, Fat 1.8g, Carbs 17.5g, Sugars 3g, Protein 3.5g

Cheesy Chicken and Broccoli Casserole

Prep Time: 25mins, Cooking Time: 45mins, Servings: 8

Ingredients

- 3 - Cups Shredded Cooked Chicken Breast
- 5 - Cups Chopped Fresh Broccoli
- 8 - oz. Cream Cheese Softened
- 1 - Cup Sour Cream, ½ - Cup Mayonnaise
- 1 - Teaspoon Garlic Salt
- 1 - Teaspoon Onion Powder, ½ - Teaspoon Basil
- ¼ - Teaspoon Smoked Paprika
- ¼ - Teaspoon Rosemary, ¼ - Teaspoon Thyme
- 1 - Cup Shredded Cheese I used Mozzarella, but you can use any kind

Instructions

- Preheat broiler to 350.
- In a vast blending bowl, consolidate all fixings aside from destroyed cheddar.
- Pour blend into a 9x13 skillet and best with 1 container destroyed cheddar.
- Prepare for 30-35 minutes, or until cheddar just begins to dark colored.

Nutrition Information: Calories 349g, Fat 12.5g, Carbs 14.4g, Sugars 1.9g, Protein 44.5g

LOW CARB CROCK POT PIZZA CASSEROLE

Prep Time: 55mins, Cooking Time: 2hrs 30mins, Servings: 6

Ingredients

- 1 - pound ground pork
- 1 - pound ground beef
- 2 - tablespoon pizza seasoning
- 1 - cup diced peppers onions, olives, mushrooms or other pizza toppings
- 1 - can diced tomatoes drained
- 1 - jar pizza sauce
- 2 - cups shredded mozzarella cheese
- 30 - pepperoni slices

Instructions

- Dark colored ground meats with seasonings with pizza flavoring over medium warmth.
- Include veggies or pizza garnishes other than pepperoni for 2-3 minutes till dampness is cooked out. Blend in depleted diced tomatoes.
- Pour meat into the goulash simmering pot. Spread out over the slow cooker.
- Pour sauce over meat and spread out equitably.
- Sprinkle equitably with cheddar.
- Top with pepperonis. You have two additional items - appreciate inspecting.
- Put the top on and cook for two hours on high or 3-4 hours on low.

Nutrition Information: Calories 309.3g, Fat 13.1g, Carbs 28.5g, Sugars 4.6g, Protein 17.8g

Low carb cauliflower rice mushroom risotto

Prep Time: 15mins, Cooking Time: 35mins, Servings: 4

INGREDIENTS

- 2 - tablespoons butter
- 2 - tablespoons olive oil
- 6 - cloves garlic, minced
- 1 - small onion, diced
- 1 - large shallot, minced
- 8 - ounces cremini mushrooms, thinly sliced
- 2 - cup chicken stock, divided
- 4 - cups riced cauliflower
- 1 - cup heavy cream
- ½ - cup grated Parmesan cheese
- 2 - tablespoons chopped fresh flat-leaf parsley
- Sea salt and black pepper, to taste

INSTRUCTIONS

- In a big sauté container, heat the spread and olive oil over medium warmth. To the skillet, including the garlic, onion, and shallot. Sauté until the onions are delicate and translucent and the garlic is fragrant. Around 5 minutes.
- To the skillet, including the mushrooms and 1 glass chicken stock. Sauté until mushrooms are delicate and have discharged their fluid. Around 5 minutes.
- Include the cauliflower and remaining 1 measure of chicken stock and blending much of the time, sauté for 10 minutes.
- Lessen the warmth to low, mix in the overwhelming cream, Parmesan cheddar, parsley, salt, and pepper. Let stew for 10 to 15 minutes to thicken.

Nutrition Information: Calories 287g, Fat 25g, Carbs 6g, Sugars 2g, Protein 10g

keto chili dog pot pie casserole

Prep Time: 25mins, Cooking Time: 30mins, Servings: 11

INGREDIENTS

- 1 - batch Slow Cooker Kickin' Chili
- 2 - tbsp butter
- 8 - grass-fed beef hot dogs, sliced
- 1 ½ - cups shredded sharp cheddar cheese
- 1 ½ - cups shredded mozzarella cheese
- 1 - batch Low Carb Cheddar Biscuit Dough (minus the sausage)

INSTRUCTIONS

- Set up the stew early. You can radically decrease the cook time of this formula by changing over the bean stew to a stovetop formula.
- Warmth the spread in a huge ovenproof skillet over medium warmth. When the spread is liquefied and the dish is hot, add the cut wieners to the container and cook until they have a decent singe on them.
- Pour the whole clump of bean stew over the cooked wieners.
- Blend the cheddar and mozzarella cheeses and sprinkle them over best of the bean stew.
- Set up the scone mixture as indicated by the headings (less the hotdog)
- Preheat broiler to 350°
- Drop vast scoops of the bread mixture over the meal.

- Heat for 30 minutes or until the bread topping is brilliant darker.

Nutrition Information: Calories 139g, Fat 11g, Carbs 7g, Sugars 2g, Protein 3g

Keto honey mustard chicken

Prep Time: 35mins, Cooking Time: 1hr 30mins, Servings: 4

INGREDIENTS

- 4 - boneless skinless chicken breasts
- 1 - cup Keto Honey Mustard Dressing, divided
- 2 - tablespoons olive oil

INSTRUCTIONS

- Join the chook and 1/2 degree of the nectar mustard dressing in a bowl and hurl the chicken, covering it within the dressing. Let marinate within the fridge for 60mins, or so long as 24 hours.
- Preheat the stove to 350°F.
- Warmth the olive oil in a big stove-proof skillet over medium-high warm temperature. When the skillet is hot, include the chook, and dish singe, sautéing on the two sides. Around 3 to 4 minutes on each facet.
- Pour the staying nectar mustard dressing over the bird. Move the skillet to the broiler and heat for 20mins or until the fowl is cooked properly.

Nutrition Information: Calories 156.1g, Fat 5.7g, Carbs 5.6g, Sugars 4.9g, Protein 17.4g

Acorn Squash with Spiced Applesauce

Prep Time: 25mins, Cooking Time: 30mins, Servings: 6

INGREDIENTS

- 1 - squash Acorn Winter Squash
- 5 - tsp Unsalted Butter Stick, ½ - tsp Salt
- ½ - tsp Black Pepper, ¾ - cup Applesauce
- 1/8 - tsp Cinnamon
- 1 - tbsp Sugar Free Maple Flavored Syrup

INSTRUCTIONS

- Preheat stove to 350°F. Cut squash down the middle, expel seeds and after that cut into 6 wedges.
- Line a sheet dish with aluminum foil. Dissolve 1 tablespoon margarine and brush on squash; sprinkle with salt and pepper.
- Spot on skillet and heat until squash is fork delicate, around 20 minutes.
- In a little pot heat the fruit purée, around 3 minutes. Mix in 2 teaspoons spread and cinnamon and cook 30 seconds more.
- Serve squash with a touch of fruit purée blend and a shower of syrup.

Nutrition Information: Calories 314.3g, Fat 5.6g, Carbs 70.3g, Sugars 0.6g, Protein 2g

Alfredo Sauce Recipe

Prep Time: 10mins, Cooking Time: 20mins, Servings: 4

INGREDIENTS

- 2 - tablespoons Unsalted Butter Stick,
- 1 ½ - cups Heavy Cream, ½ - cup Parmesan Cheese
- 4 - oz Romano Cheese, 1/8 - tsp Black Pepper
- 1/8 - tsp Nutmeg

INSTRUCTIONS

- One of the least complex and best of all pasta sauces, Alfredo sauce is sufficiently adaptable to spruce up steamed vegetables also.
- For the best flavor, purchase squares of Parmesan and Pecorino Romano and mesh them yourself.
- Liquefy spread in a medium pan over medium warmth. Include cream and stew until diminished to 1 glass, around 10 minutes.
- Mesh Parmesan and Romano cheeses.
- Expel from warmth; mix in Parmesan, Romano, pepper, and nutmeg until the cheeses have softened and sauce is smooth.
- Serve right away.
- Vodka Sauce: Prepare Alfredo Sauce as per headings, including 3 tablespoons tomato glue and 2 tablespoons vodka to the substantial cream before diminishing.

Nutrition Information: Calories 124.5g, Fat 6.4g, Carbs 7.8g, Sugars 1.2g, Protein 9.7g

Almond & Coconut Flour Muffin in a Mug

Prep Time: 25mins, Cooking Time: 35mins, Servings: 2

INGREDIENTS

- 2 - tbsp Almond Meal Flour
- 1/3 - tbsp Organic High Fiber Coconut Flour
- 1 - teaspoon Sucralose Based Sweetener
- ½ - tsp Cinnamon
- ¼ - tsp Baking Powder
- 1/8 - tsp Salt
- 1 - large Egg
- 1 - tsp Extra Virgin Olive Oil

INSTRUCTIONS

- Spot every single dry fixing in an espresso cup. Mix to join.
- Include the egg and oil. Blend until altogether joined.
- Microwave for 1 minute. Utilize a blade if important to help expel the biscuit from the container, cut, spread, and eat.

Nutrition Information: Calories 204.6g, Fat 18.4g, Carbs 8.1g, Sugars 0.4g, Protein 6.1g

Parmesan & Almond Flour Pizza Crust Recipe

Time: Prep Time: 55mins, Cooking Time: 45mins, Servings: 8

INGREDIENTS

- 1 - large Egg
- ¼ - cup Tap Water
- 1 - tablespoon Extra Virgin Olive Oil
- 1 ½ - cups Blanched Almond Flour
- ½ - cup Parmesan Cheese
- ½ - tsp Baking Powder
- ½ - tsp Xylitol
- ¾ - tsp Oregano
- ¾ - tsp Basil
- ¼ - tsp Crushed Red Pepper Flakes

INSTRUCTIONS

- This formula is appropriate for all stages with the exception of the initial two weeks of Induction because of the nuts.
- Whisk together the wet fixings in a little bowl. Put aside.
- Join the staying dry fixings; mixing to mix. The flavors are discretionary however add an incredible flavor to the batter.
- Consider signifying 1/2 tsp garlic powder just as the 1/4 tsp stew pepper chips. Add the wet fixings blending to shape a thick mixture.
- Oil two sheets of material and fold the mixture between the sheets into a flimsy circle or square to fit a pizza skillet or preparing sheet.
- Prepare at 375°F for 20-25 minutes until brilliant and fresh around the edges. Permit to cool around 20 minutes to frame a crunchy outside layer.
- Top with fixings and spot back in the stove or grill for a couple of minutes to cook the garnishes. Makes 8 cuts.

Nutrition Information: Calories 400.1g, Fat 33.6g, Carbs 12g, Sugars 2g, Protein 14.7g

Almond Muffin in a Mug Recipe

Prep Time: 30mins, Cooking Time: 35mins, Servings: 2

INGREDIENTS

- ¼ - cup Bob's Red Mill Almond Meal
- 1 - tsp No Calorie Sweetener
- ¼ - tsp Baking Powder
- 1 - dash Salt
- ½ - tsp Cinnamon
- 1 - large Egg
- 1 - tsp Canola Vegetable Oil

INSTRUCTIONS

- Spot every single dry fixing in an espresso cup. Blend to consolidate.
- Include the egg and oil. Mix until completely consolidated.
- Microwave for 1 minute. Utilize a blade if important to help expel the biscuit from the glass, cut, spread, and eat.

Nutrition Information: Calories 237.6g, Fat 18.1g, Carbs 12.3g, Sugars 0.1g, Protein 12.4g

Almond Thin and Crispy Pizza Crust

Prep Time: 35mins, Cooking Time: 50mins, Servings: 2

INGREDIENTS

- ½ - cup Tap Water
- 1 - tablespoon Extra Virgin Olive Oil
- 1 ½ - cups Almond Meal Flour
- 3 - tbsp Potato Starch
- 1 - tsp Baking Powder
- ¼ - tsp Salt
- ½ - tsp Xylitol
- ¾ - tsp leaf Oregano
- ¾ - tsp leaf Basil
- 3 - servings Organic 100% Whole Ground Golden Flaxseed Meal
- ¼ - tsp Crushed Red Pepper Flakes
- 5 - tbsp Flax seeds

INSTRUCTIONS

- This formula makes an awesome covering. It is viewed as a Phase 4 formula because of the potato starch despite the fact that it is a low sum.
- The potato starch enables the batter to extend somewhat more and to turn out to be increasingly fresh.
- Whisk together the water and oil in a little bowl. Put aside.
- Consolidate the staying dry fixings; mixing to mix. The flavors are discretionary yet include a pleasant flavor. Consider signifying 1/2 tsp garlic powder too.

- Oil two sheets of material and fold the mixture between them into a flimsy circle or square to fit a pizza container or heating sheet.
- Prepare at 375°F for 20-25 minutes until brilliant and fresh around the edges. Permit to cool around 20 minutes to frame a crunchy outside layer.
- Top with fixings and spot back in the stove or oven for a couple of minutes to cook the garnishes. Makes 8 cuts.

Nutrition Information: Calories 303.6g, Fat 23.8g, Carbs 7.4g, Sugars 0.3g, Protein 18.5g

Ancho Chili Recipe

Prep Time: 30mins, Cooking Time: 30mins, Servings: 6

INGREDIENTS

- 5 - lbs Beef Top Sirloin
- 2 - tsp Salt
- ½ - tsp Black Pepper
- 3 - tablespoons Extra Virgin Olive Oil
- 1 - medium Onions
- 4 - cloves Garlic
- 3 - tbsp Chili Powder
- 14 ½ - oz Red Tomatoes
- 6 - fl oz Red Table Win

INSTRUCTIONS

- Cooking vanishes liquor, which is the reason this formula is appropriate for Induction in spite of the red wine.
- Jostled cooked garlic cloves can be found in the product segment of most stores or just mince an entire clove of garlic.
- Warmth broiler to 325°F.
- Season hamburger with salt and pepper. Warmth 1/2 teaspoons oil in a Dutch broiler over high warmth.
- Include 33% of the hamburger and darker on all sides
- Exchange to a bowl and rehash two additional occasions with hamburger and oil.
- Slash the onion and add to a Dutch broiler preheated with the rest of the 1/2 teaspoons oil.
- Finely mince the garlic, add it to the container and cook with the onion until sautéed.
- Blend in bean stew powder, tomatoes, and wine; convey to a stew.
- Spread and prepare 2 1/2 hours, mixing once partially through cooking time, until meat is delicate.
- One serving is around 3/4-1 glass.

Nutrition Information: Calories 300g, Fat 15g, Carbs 30g, Sugars 4g, Protein 12g

Almond-Raspberry Cupcakes

Prep Time: 30mins, Cooking Time: 40mins, Servings: 12

INGREDIENTS

- 2 - large Eggs
- ¼ - cup Unsalted Butter Stick
- 1/3 - cup Sucralose Based Sweetener
- 2 - tbsp Heavy Cream
- 1 - fl oz Tap Water
- ½ - tsp Fresh Lemon Juice
- 1 - tsp Vanilla Extract
- 2 - tsp Pure Almond Extract
- 2 ½ - cups Almond Meal Flour
- ½ - tsp Baking Powder
- ½ - tsp Salt

INSTRUCTIONS

- Preheat stove to 350°F. Spot 10 paper mugs in a biscuit container and put aside. In a little bowl beat the egg yolks with 1/4 glass sucralose, spread, cream, water, lemon juice or vinegar and concentrates until completely joined.
- In another bowl beat the egg whites until foamy, include the rest of the 2 tablespoons of sucralose and keep on beating until hardened pinnacles structure.
- In a different bowl, consolidate the almond dinner, preparing powder and salt. Delicately overlap into the egg blend.
- Gap this hitter similarly between the biscuit containers at that point drop 1 teaspoon of raspberry jam into the middle.
- Prepare for 20-30 minutes until a toothpick embedded in the inside tells the truth. Permit to cool in the search for gold minutes.
- Appreciate warm or at room temperature. Refrigerate remaining cupcakes in a hermetically sealed compartment for up t0 multi-week and serve at room temperature. These may likewise be solidified for as long as multi-month.

Nutrition Information: Calories 259.4g, Fat 15g, Carbs 26.5g, Sugars 12.8g, Protein 2.9g

Arugula, Pear and Hazelnut Salad

Prep Time: 35mins, Cooking Time: 20mins, Servings: 4

INGREDIENTS

- 40 - nuts Hazelnuts or Filberts, 10 - oz Arugula
- ½ - cup, crumbled Gorgonzola Cheese
- 1 - pear, medium Pears, 2 - servings Maple-Dijon Vinaigrette

INSTRUCTIONS

- Utilize the Atkins formula to make Maple-Dijon Vinaigrette for this formula.
- You will require 4 tablespoons or 1/4 glass. This plate of mixed greens is scrumptiously presented with salmon.
- Toast hazelnuts in a dry skillet for around 15 minutes or toast on a sheet container in a stove at 350°F; permit chilling and delicately scouring external skin, coarsely slashing, and putting aside.
- Make the Maple-Dijon Vinaigrette and hurl 4 tablespoons with the arugula and Gorgonzola cheddar.
- Orchestrate the pear cuts in a fan on top and sprinkle with hazelnuts.

Nutrition Information: Calories 197.1g, Fat 12.1g, Carbs 21.3g, Sugars 15.9g, Protein 3.5g

Asian Lobster Salad

Prep Time: 25mins, Cooking Time: 20mins, Servings: 2

INGREDIENTS

- ¾ - lb Northern Lobster
- 2 - cup, shreddeds Chinese Cabbage (Bok-Choy, Pak-Choi)
- ½ - small Sweet Red Pepper
- 4 - medium (4-1/8" long) Scallions or Spring Onions
- 1 - tbsp Dried Whole Sesame Seeds
- 2 - tbsp Sodium and Sugar Free Rice Vinegar
- 2 - tbsp Tamari Soybean Sauce, 1 - tsp Ginger
- 1 - tbsp Canola Vegetable Oil, 1 - tsp Sesame Oil

INSTRUCTIONS

- For the plate of mixed greens: In a substantial serving bowl, consolidate lobster, cabbage, ringer pepper, scallions, and sesame seeds.
- For the dressing: In a little bowl, whisk the rice vinegar, Tamari soy sauce, ground ginger, and the canola and sesame oils together.
- Pour dressing over a serving of mixed greens and hurl tenderly to coat.
- Season with new ground dark pepper and salt.

Nutrition Information: Calories 197.4g, Fat 11.2g, Carbs 15.1g, Sugars 5.2g, Protein 9.4g

Asparagus in Vinaigrette with Walnuts

Prep Time: 25mins, Cooking Time: 20mins, Servings: 4

INGREDIENTS

- ¼ - cup, chopped English Walnuts
- 1 - lb Asparagus
- ¼ - small Onion
- 2 - tbsp White Wine Vinegar
- 1 - tsp Dijon Mustard
- ½ - individual packet Sucralose Based Sweetener (Sugar Substitute)
- ½ - tsp Salt
- ¼ - tsp Black Pepper
- ¼ - cup Extra Virgin Olive Oil
- 4 - cups Spring Mix Salad

INSTRUCTIONS

- To toast nuts, place them on a heating sheet in a preheated 325°F stove, turning those following 3 minutes.
- Heat for another 3 to 6 minutes, checking every now and again to abstain from consuming.
- To make this dish reasonable for Induction, essentially wipe out the walnuts.
- Steam asparagus until fresh delicate, around 4-7 minutes, contingent on size. Channel and pat dry with paper towels. Put aside.
- Consolidate finely diced white onion, vinegar, mustard, sugar substitute, salt and pepper in a blending bowl. Progressively speed in oil.
- Separation lettuce on 4 plates; orchestrate asparagus on top and sprinkle with vinaigrette. Sprinkle with walnuts and extra salt and pepper, whenever wanted.

Nutrition Information: Calories 159.2g, Fat 2.5g, Carbs 2.8g, Sugars 0.2g, Protein 29.5g

Atkins Cornbread

Prep Time: 25mins, Cooking Time: 15mins, Servings: 16

INGREDIENTS

- 3 - large Eggs, 1 - cup Whole Milk
- 1/3 - cup Vegetable Oil, 2 - tablespoons Unsalted Butter Stick
- 1 - each Chipotle en Adobo, whole
- ½ - cup Whole Grain Soy Flour, 2 - oz Vital Wheat Gluten

INSTRUCTIONS

- Preheat range to 350°F.
- Fog an eight-inch rectangular making ready dish with olive oil bathes.
- In a medium bowl, beat egg, milk, oil and dissolved unfold.
- Shred the cheeses and cleave the chilies, consist of them and blend until very lots mixed.
- Include soy flour, wheat gluten and getting ready powder blending until fixings are virtually joined.
- Spread combo into the organized field. Heat till notable.
- Cool on a wire rack five to 10 minutes earlier than cutting into sixteen servings.

Nutrition Information: Calories 130g, Fat 2.5g, Carbs 25g, Sugars 3g, Protein 2g

Atkins Barbecue Chicken Supreme Pizza

Prep Time: 35mins, Cooking Time: 55mins, Servings: 4

INGREDIENTS

- 2 - cups Atkins Flour Mix (cups)
- 1 ½ - tsp Baking Powder (Straight Phosphate, Double Acting)
- ½ - tsp Salt
- 1 - packet Sucralose Based Sweetener
- 1 - cup Tap Water
- 1 - small Red Onion
- 1 - cup, cooked, diced Chicken Breast
- ½ - medium Green Sweet Pepper
- 1 - cup Whole Milk Mozzarella Cheese
- 3 - tablespoons Extra Virgin Olive Oil
- 2 - servings Barbecue Sauce

INSTRUCTIONS

- Utilize the Atkins formula to make Barbecue Sauce. This sauce flavors up the fowl.
- Make Atkins Flour Mix make the out of doors layer for this formula.
- Warmth stove to 425°F.
- Mix collectively flour combination, heating powder, salt and sugar replacement in an expansive mixing bowl.
- Include water and oil. Utilizing a wooden spoon or a spatula, join into a aggregate.
- Utilizing a spatula, expel the batter from the bowl and see on a really perfect surface daintily protected with olive oil splash.

- Coat moving a pin with oil splash and roll the aggregate out to healthy the pizza dish.
- Prepare the covering for 10mins and expel from the broiler.
- Spread Barbecue Sauce uniformly over the pizza.
- Sprinkle with mozzarella and top with chook portions, ringer pepper cuts.
- Sprinkle with salt and pepper, to flavor.
- Come again to the broiler and hold heating for 10-15 minutes.

Nutrition Information: Calories 254.6g, Fat 6.1g, Carbs 24g, Sugars 1.9g, Protein 24.8g

Atkins Pizza Dough

Prep Time: 35mins, Cooking Time: 30mins, Servings: 8

INGREDIENTS

- 1 ½ - tsp Baking Powder (Straight Phosphate, Double Acting)
- ½ - tsp Salt
- 1 1/8 - cups Tap Water
- 3 - tablespoons Extra Virgin Olive Oil
- 6 - servings Atkins Flour Mix

INSTRUCTIONS

- Utilize the Atkins formula to make Atkins Flour Mix for this formula, you will require 2 glasses.
- Spare the staying in a sealed shut compartment in the fridge for different formulas.
- Preheat broiler to 425°F.
- Mix every single dry fixing together in an expansive blending bowl.
- Include wet fixings with a spoon or spatula and join into a mixture.
- With a spatula, remove the mixture from the bowl and spot on a perfect surface daintily covered with non-stick vegetable oil shower.
- Coat moving a pin with a non-stick splash and roll the batter out to fit the pizza dish.
- It might be simpler to utilize your hands.
- The pre-heat outside layer at 425°F for 10 minutes.
- Include sauce, cheddar, and extra vegetables and meats whenever wanted and warm in the broiler until cheddar softens.

Nutrition Information: Calories 380g, Fat 25g, Carbs 28g, Sugars 2g, Protein 23g

Cajun Chicken with Okra

Prep Time: 25mins, Cooking Time: 55mins, Servings: 4

INGREDIENTS

- 3 - tbsp Whole Grain Soy Flour
- ¾ - tsp Salt
- ¼ - tsp Black Pepper
- 24 - oz Chicken Thigh, boneless, with skin
- 2 - tsp Canola Vegetable Oil
- 1 ¾ - cups Tomatoes, red, ripe, canned, with green chilies
- 2/3 - cup Chicken Broth, Bouillon or Consomme
- 1 - oz Garlic
- ¼ - tsp Crushed Red Pepper Flakes
- ½ - tsp Tabasco Sauce
- 1 10 - oz frozen package yield Cooked Okra

INSTRUCTIONS

- Spot soy flour, 1/2 teaspoon salt, and pepper in a plastic sack. Add chicken pieces and shake to coat. Put aside.
- Warmth oil in a huge nonstick skillet over high warmth until hot. Include chicken and sauté until cooked on all sides, around 5 minutes.
- Include tomatoes with their juices, minced garlic, juices, 1/4 teaspoon salt and pepper, squashed red pepper pieces and red pepper sauce.
- Heat to the point of boiling, spread decrease warmth to low and stew 10 to 15 minutes until chicken is cooked through.

- Include okra, spread, and stew until okra is delicate, around 5 minutes.

Nutrition Information: Calories 125.5g, Fat 4.8g, Carbs 16g, Sugars 1.4g, Protein 8.2g

Deviled-Egg Coleslaw

Prep Time: 25mins, Cooking Time: 20mins, Servings: 12

INGREDIENTS

- 2 - large Boiled Eggs
- ¾ - cup Real Mayonnaise
- 3 - tbsp Dijon Mustard
- 3 -tbsp chopped Onions
- 1 - tbsp Distilled White Vinegar
- ¼ - tsp Original Pepper Sauce
- 1 - tsp Salt
- ¼ - tsp Old Bay Seasoning
- 8 - cup, shreddeds Cabbage

INSTRUCTIONS

- Consolidate hacked eggs, mayonnaise, mustard, white onion, vinegar, hot sauce, salt, and flavoring in a substantial bowl.
- Include cabbage, and hurl well.
- Spread, and chill for something like 1 hour before serving.

Nutrition Information: Calories 55.1g, Fat 2.7g, Carbs 3.5g, Sugars 1.5g, Protein 3.3g

Deviled Eggs

Prep Time: 20mins, Cooking Time: 25mins, Servings: 14

INGREDIENTS

- 6 - large Boiled Eggs, 2 - tbsp Celery
- 1 - medium Scallions or Spring Onions
- 2 - oz boneless, cooked Fresh Ham
- 1 1/3 - tbsp, taineds Capers, 3 - tbsp Real Mayonnaise
- 1 - tsp Dijon Mustard

INSTRUCTIONS

- Cut the same eggs down the middle the long way; scoop out yolks into a bowl.
- Bones the celery, onion and ham and spot in the bowl with yolks.
- Include the tricks, mayonnaise, and mustard blending to consolidate and season to taste with salt and pepper.
- Gap the yolk blend equitably among the saved whites, mounding it marginally.
- Trimming with paprika and parsley whenever wanted.
- Eggs might be put away, canvassed in plastic in the icebox for as long as 1 day.

Nutrition Information: Calories 145g, Fat 13g, Carbs 0.5g, Sugars 0.5g, Protein 6.5g

Fried Green Tomatoes

Prep Time: 25mins, Cooking Time: 35mins, Servings: 6

INGREDIENTS

- 4 - medium Green Tomatoes
- 1/3 - cup Yellow Whole Grain Corn Flour
- ½ - tsp Salt, ¼ - tsp Black Pepper
- 3 - tbsp Canola Vegetable Oil
- 1 - serving Atkins Flour Mix

INSTRUCTIONS

- Utilize the Atkins formula to make Atkins Flour Mix for this formula, you will require 1/3 glass.
- Cut tomatoes across into 1/2 thick cuts. In a shallow plate consolidate cornmeal, heating blend, salt, and pepper.
- Warmth oil in an extensive nonstick skillet over medium-high warmth.
- Dig 4 to 5 of the tomato cuts and sear 2 minutes for every side, until brilliant. Rehash this procedure, cleaning skillet between bunches.

Nutrition Information: Calories 140g, Fat 7.7g, Carbs 13.5g, Sugars 3g, Protein 4.7g

Garden Frittata

Prep Time: 35mins, Cooking Time: 30mins, Servings: 4

INGREDIENTS

- 3 - tablespoons Extra Virgin Olive Oil
- 2 - each Leeks
- ¼ - head, large Cauliflower
- 5 - Whole each Mushroom Pieces and Stems
- 8 - large Eggs
- 2 - tbsp Basil
- ½ - tsp Rosemary (Dried)
- 3 - tbsp Parmesan Cheese

INSTRUCTIONS

- Preheat oven. Clean and plan leeks, cut the white part just into think cuts.
- Coarsely hack the cauliflower and cut the mushrooms.
- Warmth oil in a medium ovenproof skillet over medium warmth.
- Include leeks and cauliflower; sauté until fresh delicate, around 10 minutes.
- Include mushrooms; cook 5 minutes, until mushrooms start to emit fluid.
- Lessen warmth to low. Empty eggs into skillet, blending marginally.
- Include basil and rosemary, alongside salt and pepper to taste.
- Cook, blending every now and again until eggs start to shape little curds and set.
- Include cheddar and daintily press into egg blend with a spatula.
- Spot skillet under oven; cook until top is set however not dark-colored, around 1 minute.
- To expel frittata entire, tip skillet to the other side and utilize a spatula to slacken edges.

Nutrition Information: Calories 166.4g, Fat 9.5g, Carbs 4.4g, Sugars 3.1g, Protein 14.4g

Ham and Cheese Roll-Ups

Prep Time: 35mins, Cooking Time: 33mins, Servings: 8

INGREDIENTS

- 6 - thin slice Fresh Ham
- 6 - slice Swiss Cheese
- 6 - spears Pickles
- 2 - tbsp Real Mayonnaise
- 2 - tbsp Dijon Mustard

INSTRUCTIONS

- Trim ham, cheddar, and pickles to meet lengths. Spread out ham cuts, top with cheddar cuts.
- Join mayo and mustard; spread onto cheddar. Lay pickle in focus and move up firmly.
- Cut into nibble estimated pieces.

Nutrition Information: Calories 187.1g, Fat 6.9g, Carbs 18.3g, Sugars 1g, Protein 12g

Herb Roasted Chicken with Lemon

Prep Time: 35mins, Cooking Time: 40mins, Servings: 6

INGREDIENTS

- 1 - tsp Salt
- ¼ - tsp Black Pepper
- 2 - tsp Thyme
- 1 - fruit Lemon
- ¾ - cup Chicken Broth
- 2 - tablespoons Unsalted Butter Stick
- 48 - oz Whole Chicken

INSTRUCTIONS

- Warmth broiler to 350°F.
- Sprinkle bird with salt, pepper, and herb, all around.
- Relax pores and skin from bosom with a pointer, and stuff 2 cups of lemon and 1 tablespoon spread onto every side of the bosom.
- Spot remaining lemon in the hollow.
- Exchange bird to a simmering dish.
- A moment meat thermometer must peruse 170°F within the thickest piece of the thigh.
- Exchange bird to a reducing board; keep up 10 minutes earlier than reducing to permit juices to redistribute.
- Spot skillet more than 2 broiler burners; pour in hen soup and warmth to the factor of boiling.
- Rub up dark-colored bits on the bottom of skillet.
- Cook 2-3 minutes. Pour over cut chook.

Nutrition Information: Calories 194.6g, Fat 6.6g, Carbs 3g, Sugars 0.1g, Protein 29.2g

Baby Spinach, Pickled Beets and Tomato Salad

Prep Time: 35mins, Cooking Time: 20mins, Servings: 8

INGREDIENTS

- 1 ½ - cups Baby Spinach
- ¼ - cup, sliced Pickled Beets
- 5 - Cherry Tomatoes

INSTRUCTIONS

- Spot the spinach leaves in a bowl. Include beets and tomatoes and tenderly prepare with low-carb serving of mixed greens dressing of your decision.
- Season to taste with salt and crisply ground dark pepper.

Nutrition Information: Calories 290.5g, Fat 18.3g, Carbs 22.8g, Sugars 1.7g, Protein 11.9g

Bacon-Egg Salad Flat-out Wrap

Prep Time: 15mins, Cooking Time: 25mins, Servings: 4

INGREDIENTS

- 2 - large Boiled Eggs
- 1 - tbsp Real Mayonnaise
- ½ - tsp or 1 packet Yellow Mustard
- 1 - flatbread Light Original Flatbread
- 1 ½ - oz, cookeds Turkey Bacon
- 1 - Inner leaf Romaine Lettuce (salad)

INSTRUCTIONS

- Combine slashed eggs, mayonnaise, and mustard. Add salt and pepper to taste.
- Spread blend on one adjusted end of Flat that has the lettuce straightened out on it.
- Top with cooked crushed bacon at that point move up and cut down the middle.

Nutrition Information: Calories 390g, Fat 27g, Carbs 25g, Sugars 2g, Protein 12g

Caesar Salad

Prep Time: 30mins, Cooking Time: 25mins, Servings: 4

INGREDIENTS

- 4 - tbsp Real Mayonnaise
- 1 - tbsp Anchovy Paste
- 1 - tbsp Lemon Juice
- 1 - tablespoon Extra Virgin Olive Oil
- ½ - tbsp Worcestershire Sauce
- 1 - tsp Garlic
- 1 - tsp Dijon Mustard
- ¼ - tsp Salt
- ¼ - tsp Black Pepper
- 1/8 - tsp Tabasco Sauce
- 7 - tbsp Parmesan Cheese
- 1 - head Cos or Romaine Lettuce
- 8 - each Anchovy

INSTRUCTION

- Generally, Caesar plate of mixed greens is supplied with bread garnishes.
- When you are in Phase 2, you could pinnacle this plate of mixed greens with low carb bread garnishes.
- Spread on a getting ready sheet and warmth in a preheated 350°F broiler for 6 - 8mins until top-notch is darker.
- In a little bowl, whisk mayonnaise, anchovy glue, lemon juice, oil, Worcestershire sauce, minced garlic, mustard,

salt, pepper and a sprinkle of Tabasco until easy. Blend in three tablespoons of the cheddar.

- Hurl lettuce with dressing until equitably included.
- Separation on plates; top with wonderful cheddar and 2 anchovies for each plate.
- Serve finished with chook, salmon or shrimp to make it a complete dinner party.

Nutrition Information: Calories 150g, Fat 13g, Carbs 7g, Sugars 2g, Protein 4g

CONCLUSION

The Atkins Diet is by all accounts a viable method for getting more fit for some individuals. Be that as it may, eating a low-starch and high-protein diet has various consequences for various frameworks in the body.

A low-sugar diet may likewise profit those with scatters, for example, type 2 diabetes and polycystic ovary disorder. In these conditions, one of the issues is the manner in which the body forms sugars and the substance (hormone) called insulin. Frequently they find getting in shape by following a conventional low-fat eating regimen especially troublesome.

Manufactured by Amazon.ca
Bolton, ON

29597732R00070